If you've ever had questions about how relevant God's Word is to your life, you need this book. Michael and Lauren not only understand your hesitations but come alongside you to process your questions while uncovering the ways Scripture can become a personal lifeline.

—**LYSA TERKEURST,** #1 *New York Times* bestselling author; president, Proverbs 31 Ministries

Lauren and Michael offer in this accessible work a hopeful vision for millennials and gen Zers who are skeptical of the Bible's claims. May this book encourage you to read and consider with an open mind the most important book in history.

—**RUSSELL MOORE,** president, The Ethics and Religious Liberty Commission of the Southern Baptist Convention

Engaging. Timely. This book invites skeptics and seekers alike to a renewed understanding and embrace of God's Word. Michael and Lauren are wise and trustworthy guides, encouraging us to find our story within the greatest story of all.

—**LOUIE GIGLIO,** pastor, Passion City Church; founder, Passion Conferences

Lauren and Michael have been friends with my wife and me for some years. Their willingness to listen and welcome challenging perspectives tells me a lot about their character. They value truth over their biases and aren't afraid of the uncomfortable questions. That is why they are so well equipped to share what they've found in this book.

—**ANDY MINEO,** hip-hop recording artist

Not only millennials but readers from every generation will benefit from this fresh perspective on the Bible. This book creates space for the skeptical or casual Bible reader to address the hard questions head on. We need that now more than ever.

—**GABE LYONS,** president, Q Ideas; author, *Good Faith*

Conversational, clear, compelling, convincing—here's a winsome and insightful invitation to experience the most profound and controversial book of history. Are you willing to read this book by the McAfees with an open mind? If so, great surprises—and rewards—await you.

—**LEE STROBEL,** bestselling author, *The Case for Christ* and *The Case for Miracles*

If you are a millennial who has never considered the Bible, drop everything and read this book. Michael and Lauren dare you to see things
you may have overlooked about the most popular book in history.

—**ERIC METAXAS,** #1 *New York Times* bestselling author;
host, nationally syndicated *The Eric Metaxas Radio Show*

Michael and Lauren offer historical, biblical, and practical advice for
their generation and future generations to come. You will walk away
with a better understanding of the millennial and gen Z generations,
and your love for the Bible will deepen in the process.

—**ROBBY AND KANDI GALLATY,** authors,
Here and Now and *Disciple Her*

This book invites the millennial generation to shake off their precon-
ceptions about the Bible and explore its pages for themselves. Michael
and Lauren provide thoughtful encouragement in this welcome read.

—**BOBBY GRUENEWALD,** founder, YouVersion Bible App

I encourage you to order a stack of copies of this book and pass them
to young people in your life that you care about, as well as reading
it for yourself. Together, we can reconnect the next generation with
the Word of God.

—**MATT BROWN,** evangelist, author,
founder of Think Eternity

Michael and Lauren are a much needed voice for biblical inerrancy
in the millennial generation. They challenge all of us to face our
questions about the Bible head on and not to dismiss the Bible before
reading it. Any of us who care to see our faith transferred to the next
generation must read this book.

—**ESTHER FLEECE ALLEN,** speaker;
author, *No More Faking Fine*

The McAfees have articulated an insightful and helpful explanation of
how millennials are colliding with the Book of All Books. It will help
you, as it helped me, to gain a greater understanding of millennials
in your congregation and community.

—**DR. CHRIS WALL,** senior pastor, First Baptist
Church of Owasso, Oklahoma

NOT

WHAT

YOU

THINK

NOT WHAT YOU THINK

WHY THE BIBLE MIGHT BE
NOTHING WE EXPECTED YET
EVERYTHING WE NEED

MICHAEL & LAUREN MCAFEE

ZONDERVAN

Not What You Think
Copyright © 2019 by Michael McAfee and Lauren Green McAfee

Requests for information should be addressed to:
Zondervan, *3900 Sparks Dr. SE, Grand Rapids, Michigan 49546*

ISBN 978-0-310-35521-2 (hardcover)

ISBN 978-0-310-35523-6 (audio)

ISBN 978-0-310-35522-9 (ebook)

The authors are represented by the literary agency of Alive Communications, Inc., 7680 Goddard Street, Suite 200, Colorado Springs, Colorado 80920, www .aliveliterary.com.

Cover design: Faceout Studio
Cover photos: Tamisclao / Shutterstock
Interior design: Kait Lamphere

Printed in the United States of America

19 20 21 22 23 24 25 /LSC/ 15 14 13 12 11 10 9 8 7 6 5 4 3 2 1

For Mom

<(o)> <3 U

—*Michael*

To Mom and Dad,

without whom this book

could not exist (literally)

—*Lauren*

CONTENTS

PART 1:
Who We Are:
The Shaping of Millennials

PART 2:
Where We Are From:
The Bible and History

PART 3:

Where We Are Going:

The Millennial Mind on the Bible

PART 4:

How We Get There:

The Starting Point

FOREWORD

You have in your hands a unique book.

First, it is unique because of who is writing it. There is more skepticism toward the Bible among young people today than there has been in any previous generation in our nation's history. There are certainly books written by older authors who (usually rather sternly) lecture younger adults regarding the attitude they ought to have toward Scripture. What we have not had is a volume like this one. It is written by two who are millennials themselves and so are immersed in their generation's experiences and culture, who have wrestled with their own relationship to the Bible, and who have emerged to introduce the Bible to their peers with fresh and hard-won appreciation for it.

Second, it is unique because it is several books in one. You can certainly find books on the cultural characteristics of the millennial generation. You can also get good books—and very big and long ones—on how to answer common objections to the trustworthiness of the Bible, on the basic teachings of the Bible, on how to read and interpret the Bible, and on how the Bible can be a foundation for spiritual experience of God. The McAfees have read many of these. They have brought many of their seminal insights together and expressed them in the most accessible way. And they address the concerns and questions that millennials would have with it all.

Finally, Michael and Lauren do not examine the Bible in an academic way but connect it closely to Jesus himself. It is a book about Jesus and it is the book of Jesus.

In a class I teach, I ask my Christian students to each interview a friend who does not believe in Christianity. Two of the interview questions are, What to you is the most attractive thing about Christianity? and, What to you is the least attractive or most objectionable thing about Christianity? As might be guessed, the most problematic issue is the behavior of the church in various times and places in history. The most attractive thing to the interviewees, however, is Jesus, his character and teaching.

As the McAfees observe, millennials are turned off to the Bible because they are turned off by the church. The remedy for that is not, of course, to make any excuses for the church. Rather, millennials will be helped the most in their attitude toward the Bible if they see the strength of the connection between the Bible and Jesus.

If you read the accounts of Jesus' life in the Gospels, you will see that almost ten percent of his statements are quotes from Scripture. You will also see that Jesus didn't just talk about Scripture in a detached, philosophical manner. When he encounters Satan in the wilderness, he uses Scripture. When he is facing arrest and torture, he's quoting Scripture. When he is dying in agony, he quotes Psalm 22:1: "My God, my God. Why have you forsaken me?" Jesus did not merely believe in the authority of Scripture; he lived it. With it, he made every decision, interpreted every event, and got the strength to face every challenge. It was the mainspring of his life. Everything was understood through the grid of Scripture. Everything was done through the power of Scripture.

What does this mean? It means that it would be impossible to embrace Jesus and reject the basis for everything he believed and did. To respect Jesus, you must respect Scripture, and to make Jesus the basis of your life, you must accept the basis of his. Michael and Lauren make this case in a winsome and lucid way. This is a book we need.

—*Tim Keller*

A WORD TO
NON-MILLENNIALS

From the time George Washington was sworn in as our first president, the United States has by and large had a love affair with the Holy Bible. For the vast majority of our nation's history, the Bible has been dominant in affection and unrivaled in influence. With the recent sharp rise in skepticism leading many to hostility toward the Book of Books, it is likely that there are more Bible skeptics living in America today than in all previous generations combined. With Bible hostility on the rise, at the center of the confusion is the young adult generation—millennials and generation Z.

Unashamedly, we wrote this book to millennials and generation Z. They have come of age at the dawn of the internet. While the technology age has brought about a wealth of new information, we believe that something was lost in the transition from analog to digital: the Bible's timeless message. As millennials ourselves, this book is a plea to our peers not to dismiss the Bible before giving it a fair chance.

Although this book is aimed at young adults, it is also for

parents, pastors, and anyone who cares about future generations. Our hope is that it will become a resource for you to better understand us. Along with growing your compassion for the largest generation in American history, we hope also to equip you to recognize why we have real problems with the Bible before dismissing our reservations as immature and uninformed.

Millennials have become the punchline of countless jokes. This should not come as a surprise. Every generation goes through a season of hazing when they are ostracized for their youth, a rite of passage as the established generations bemoan the changes in the world around them and blame the children they raised for the perceived decline in culture. With this comes frustration both for millennials who are trying to make their own way in this world and for non-millennials who don't understand the paths we've chosen to take.

This book is an appeal to young adults from young adults, for us to reconsider our place in the world and the Bible's place in ours. Many books have been written to appeal to young adults to reconsider their views on organized religion, especially Christianity. We want to have a conversation about Christianity, the church, and Jesus himself, but we are content here to focus on the Bible. Why? We believe that if we read the Bible for ourselves, we might find that it is nothing we expected, yet everything we need.

ACKNOWLEDGMENTS

There are far too many people to thank in a brief acknowledgments page. First, our families who have raised us and supported us in all things. We love you and we like you. Second, our church family, Council Road, and the pastors, leaders, and people who over the years have invested countless hours in our spiritual formation. We couldn't imagine life without this community. Thanks to our employers, Hobby Lobby and Museum of the Bible, and the leaders at both of these organizations, who love the Bible. It is an honor to work alongside of you. We are grateful to God for the Southern Baptist Theological Seminary community and the many professors and leaders there who have invested in us over the years to shape the way we think about the Scriptures. Thanks to Barna and David Kinnaman for the outstanding research which shaped many of our thoughts in this book. Thanks to Zondervan for editing and publishing this book. And thanks to countless others who have encouraged us in our writing and sharpened us with their feedback.

Finally, and most of all, thanks to Drew Griffin. When we moved to New York City, knowing almost no one, Drew became a fast friend. While doing everything from watching 4-D movies

Acknowledgments

in Manhattan to fly fishing in Oklahoma, we had countless conversations about life, our generation, the Bible, and secular culture. Drew was not only an indispensable sounding board for this book but also the cowriter of the first draft. This book would not exist without his encouragement and taking notes on things we were processing, adding more research of his own, and putting structure to our jumbled mess. Thank you for your tireless work to make this book possible. And thank you Emily and Charlotte for giving Drew space and time to escape to a monastery to finish the writing.

PART 1

WHO WE ARE

The Shaping of Millennials

CHAPTER 1

ARE WE MISSING OUT?

The unexamined life is not worth living.

—SOCRATES

The countdown began, and I (Michael) was gripped with fear. Ten. Nine. Eight.

While everything worked out fine in other places, what would be our fate?

Seven. Six.

I turned to my parents for comfort, but they had wide smiles and bright eyes as they stared at the clock.

Five. Four.

I scanned the room for help, yet no one was aware of my panic or the doom that was certain to fall on us all.

Three. Two. One.

I shut my eyes and slammed my hands to my ears as everyone around me screamed.

"Happy New Year!"

I am just one of billions of brave survivors of the Y2K almost apocalypse.

If you are a few years younger than us, you might not remember this cataclysmic event, so allow me to explain. During the 1990s, the world shifted at a breakneck pace to being run by computers and the internet, laying the foundation for some of the greatest technological advances of all time. But there was one massive oversight: every computer was programmed to record dates using a scheme of three two-digit numbers. So when the clocks were about to roll over to 01-01-00, scientists lost their minds wondering what would happen when computers weren't able to register that "00" meant 2000—not 1900, before computers even existed. The threat of a shutdown caused mass hysteria, but mainly just in the canned food aisle of your local Kmart.

The rise of technology was not immune to Ron Swanson-esque resistance from a slew of doubters from our parents' generation who did not understand the potential that technology offers us. Are there drawbacks to becoming isolated or dependent on technology? Sure. But tech curmudgeons overlooked its power to shape our lives for good. While there are some dangers of misusing technology, the internet provides us a platform to accomplish amazing things if we use it well. Yet there are still people who are blind to the good opportunities afforded us by the internet and our smartphones; they've dismissed the internet before ever engaging with it because of stereotypes formed by the abuse of the internet by a minority of users. Earlier today I attempted, yet again, to persuade my grandfather that he would enjoy Facebook. Not necessarily because we use it all that much anymore but because his friends do. At least this past year he has started to text, so that's a step in the right direction!

The global seismic shift that occurred during our lifetimes has drastically changed the way we relate to the world around us. And we're not just talking about tossing our CDs and DVDs. At our fingertips we have free access, anywhere on the planet, to nearly limitless knowledge. As of 2017, more than half of the world was internet connected. When we all survived New Year's Day in the year 2000, that number was less than 5 percent.[1]

While the rise of the internet has given us opportunities our parents never could have dreamed of, there are definitely some risks: we can suffer from information overload; we can become distracted; we can be slaves to the immediate rather than thinking for the long term; we can quickly dismiss anything that is not the latest and greatest, because newer is better!

We (Michael and Lauren) fear that something has been lost in the transition from the old internet days to the new. Something that is so foundational to our story that it is *the* story that makes sense of our story. It is the narrative within which all humankind can find their way. It is an epic that is being written through our lives. Yet we, as a generation, have disregarded the tale because we have yet to understand its power to shape our lives and our communities for good. We (Michael and Lauren) fear that our generation has dismissed the Bible before ever reading it and allowing the Book to stand or fall on its merits.

The Bible is valuable because it is not new but timeless. In the same way your grandparents or even your parents may have blown off the internet before testing it for themselves, people from our generation have rejected the Bible before giving it due consideration. This book is our appeal to you to be open-minded about the Book. Occasionally, we will use the term book to refer to the Bible. To help clarify that we are referring to the Bible and not the book you are reading, we have capitalized the word Book. Hopefully, this will help you disentangle the Book from the people who have used, misused, and abused it.

If you are adventuresome enough, we invite you to journey with us. But we ask that you come with an open mind and bring your authentic questions. We will share ours. At the end, if you do not feel the Bible is worth exploring, that's a decision we will respect. Our hope in these pages is to disentangle the Book from bad experiences with religion and church, and we freely admit these experiences are real and to be lamented. If you are game, we believe you might find the Bible is not what you expected but everything you need.

WHAT ABOUT US?

You may be wondering, "Who are these writers and why should I consider their perspective?" To start, we have a confession to make: we are biased. We are both millennials. We've both grown up around the Bible like we grew up with the Olsen twins. That doesn't mean we have always had a perfect relationship with the Book. The older we get, the more we have encountered legitimate arguments to chuck deuces to the Bible. Maybe you can relate. Between experiences with Christians who give this Book a bad name, personal experiences that raise doubt, compelling critical arguments, and a culture that pushes against many of the Bible's core tenets, it is difficult to understand why this Book should matter and how it is relevant to our lives. Yet despite the criticism the Book receives, we are pulled back in, like a Taylor Swift song you cannot stop humming. With all of its complexity, the Book holds wisdom we cannot escape. And it makes truth claims we are unable to ignore. Our hope is that you will be open-minded and committed to exploring the Bible with fresh eyes. We're not here to coerce you to share our convictions. We simply want to invite you to come and see for yourself.

Here's the thing: we are a little uncomfortable exposing our Bible loyalties before we have much of a relationship with you. The reason has nothing to do with the Book itself. If the Bible is all it claims to be, it can take all our criticism. The reason we hesitate to give a defense of the Bible is probably the same reason you are skeptical about reading the Book yourself. It has little to do with the words on the pages. The reality is, the Bible has been misused for centuries. Because it is considered a source of encouragement and advice, it has been used as a weapon to manipulate and abuse vulnerable people searching for hope.

We know we are not alone in our generation. Most of us share a complicated relationship with the Bible.

As of this writing, Lauren and I have recently crossed the threshold from our twenties into the big three-zero. We are millennials who have come of age in an era of unprecedented technological and cultural change. We share with many of you generation-defining milestones and events. Our lives have been shaped by social media, informed by the internet, marred by divorce, and impacted by religion. We are millennials writing to millennials (born 1980–1995) and our younger siblings, generation Z (born 1996–2010), as well as anyone who cares about the future of these generations and their engagement with Scripture.

That said, we know that every generation instinctively resists being branded and lumped in with others simply because of the year in which they were born. Just last week, our friend Phillip, from an older generation, asked if we could explain to him the millennials' obsession with avocado toast. We were appalled. Avocado toast is not a millennial trend, it is just tasty! Not even a week later, we were sitting at a table in a trendy coffee and brunch spot. We each took a few bites of our delicious, avocado-smothered toast before we realized the irony. Michael took an obligatory selfie and texted it to our friend. We were caught being millennials.

We've been teased by our parents for taking selfies, but once they learned how to take them, they behaved no differently. We've been judged for our hypersensitivity to FOMO, yet just like every generation, we value getting the most out of life. And we are laughed at for wanting craft coffee, but that is only until the laughers recognize that Starbucks coffee is a burnt disaster. While we appreciate the humor in all this, we also know what it's like to be stereotyped in more consequential ways because of our age. Like you, we have had to grapple with generational prejudice and miscommunication. Neither of us want to contribute to a judgmental conversation or add to the negative stereotyping of our generation. Every day we witness, in the lives and struggles of our friends and contemporaries, traits that inspire us to change the world for the better and encourage us to believe we can.

This book isn't just about the largest generation on earth today. It's also about the most influential Book in history and how the two collide. And that's where things start to get interesting.

Since 2013, we have traveled the country, speaking on behalf of the Museum of the Bible. I (Lauren) was one of the first employees of the museum. My dad, Steve Green, is founder and board chairman of the museum. When the idea for the museum was being formulated, I was completing my undergraduate degree and looking for a job. I was lucky enough to have my dad hire me for my first full-time gig, and I helped out as a curator for the newly formed museum collection.

It is not just Lauren whose career has centered on the Bible. I (Michael) showed up to my first-grade class on career day wearing a blazer and carrying a Bible. I boldly declared amid a sea of my peers wearing Michael Jordan jerseys that I would grow up not to become a professional athlete but to be a preacher. Since high school, I have held a paid job at a church in some capacity. Even now, while working full-time at Museum of the Bible, I remain a teaching pastor at the same church where I met Lauren when we were seven years old.

After a few years of both of us working at Museum of the Bible in separate departments, there was an opportunity for us to work together on a new awareness campaign. The museum was within a year of opening in Washington, D.C., and it was time to share the news and invite people to support the mission. We were thrilled at the opportunity to serve the museum in this way and work more closely together in the process. The new role meant we were traveling to a new city almost weekly. We were speaking at events, setting up booths at conferences, and sharing with communities this vision to invite all people to engage with the Bible through the museum.

During that time, we met fellow millennials and heard their stories and discovered that our generation typically falls into three camps when it comes to Bible engagement. The first group is what we will call *Bible-readers*, people who as a result of heritage or conversion hold the Bible in high regard and interact with it frequently. They are interested in the Bible to the point of reading the Bible. As you may have gathered by now, Michael and I are firmly in this first group. We met in Sunday school as children, led Bible studies as early as high school, and have read countless books about the Bible, underlined and highlighted to prove it. Don't get us wrong, we are total hypocrites most days, but we are committed to the importance of the Bible in our lives and attempt to read it daily.

While some of you might be astonished to learn that anyone in our generation would live this way—perhaps you are ready to set this book down or use it for your next campfire—we know there are a lot of you who are exactly like us. We may be a minority in our generation, but there is a quiet, flourishing remnant of twenty- and thirtysomethings loyal to the Bible and the historic Christian faith. According to the latest research, 27 percent of all millennials read the Bible at least once every week.[2]

Whether or not you are in this group, you may be surprised that so many twenty- to thirty-somethings read the Bible so frequently. This is not even counting the millennials who read less frequently but want to read the Bible more. There is a significant minority of millennials who are Bible readers. Yes, we are outliers in this sense. We have more Bibles than we have video games. We read books about the Bible more often than we attend great concerts. We have dedicated our lives to the story hidden in the pages of this book, even to the point of sacrificing nights and weekends to pursue doctoral degrees—centered on the importance of this ancient Book—and to writing the book you are reading now. We are obsessed with the Bible's amazing story. And we think that if you had a fresh perspective, you might catch a glimpse of its wonder as well.

The second group we call *Bible-open*. These are millennials who were perhaps raised around church or are familiar with Christianity and the Bible but currently have little to no inter-action with the Bible. Many of our friends are in this second group, so we get why some might disengage from the Bible. There is so much we love about this group! They represent the vast majority of our generation and have a positive or at least neutral view of the Bible.[3] Nearly two out of three millennials believe the Bible was written by God. Nearly three out of four millennials consider the Bible a holy book, and 56 percent of us agree that the Bible contains everything you need to lead a meaningful life.[4] But familiarity can lull us to sleep, like Jigglypuff on *Super Smash Bros.*, which only sets us up to be home run smashed off the screen.

The third and final group we refer to as *Bible-closed*. This group is no longer open to considering whether the Bible is a transcendent, divine word to humankind. Some have read the Bible and dismissed it. However, from our experience the vast majority of this group has dismissed the Bible based on the information provided to them from others and have not read the Bible to consider its claims for themselves. They may claim to be atheists, agnostics, spiritual, adherents of another religion, or one of the growing number of "nones" who have opted out of religious identification altogether.

It is our hope that this book will inspire conversation between members of these three groups and encourage individuals to ask questions about their interactions with the Bible.

Both of us grew up in the church, were raised by Christian parents, became Christians at an early age, and now work in Christian contexts. No book has had a greater impact on our lives than the Bible. Some of you, like us, have had similar experiences with the Bible. But we realize that to a certain extent we are outliers in our generation because we have wrestled with our doubts about the Bible and Christianity while continuing to read the Bible. Many of you read about our experience and cannot relate. The Barna Group found that in 2016, Millennials (11 percent) are half as likely as Elders (25 percent) to be Bible engaged and twice as likely to be Bible skeptics (26 percent vs. 13 percent).[5] And because they read less than previous generations, teens are even less likely to be Bible engaged (7 percent).[6]

Let's face it: for most people, the Bible is at best a curiosity, at worst a weapon of manipulation. Some of you may have little experience with the Bible, and aside from laughing at the farting preacher on YouTube or that time you accidentally started a conversation with a missionary, you may never have even read a verse or heard a line of biblical text.

We get it. There are fair reasons to be skeptical about the notion that the Bible is more than you think. The Bible is a difficult book to read. We are talking about a book that is not just vintage but *ancient*. People have been studying it for centuries and still struggle to understand some of its meaning. It was written in Hebrew, Greek, and Aramaic by various authors, from diverse contexts and backgrounds, over hundreds of years. It is a sacred text to many and a dangerous text to some. But both of us have witnessed firsthand its impact for good and firmly believe that when the Bible has been properly applied to life, it makes the world a better place. Not only has it changed the world in the past; the Bible has the power to transform our modern world as well.

But the Bible's greatest impact that we have experienced has been personal, not cultural. The Bible has shaped the world and transformed not merely life itself but billions of individual lives. It impacts people and cultures on every continent. And it has impacted our lives in countless ways we will share throughout this book. The Bible is a record of the story of human history that gives it a timeless influence on all of humanity. However, not every generation relates to its importance in the same way.

Every faith and philosophy reaches for an understanding of the mystery of God. Christianity is different: it's a faith in which God reached out to humankind. He still does. God came to us in the person of Jesus and through the testimony of his life and work found in the Bible, a work that continues to touch and shape and encourage people every moment of every day.

The Bible is a personal story set on a universal stage. While it was written in a different time and in a different language, God gave us this timeless message to speak to our story in our day. The Bible not only is set apart as a compelling tale but also claims to be *the* story about everything. Including you and me.

Let's get something straight from the start: this book is more about our questions than our answers. We are there with you, exploring and wrestling and discovering together the value of the Bible and what it might mean for your life and our lives. We are not put off by your objections and doubts. We share some as well, and throughout this book we will tell you how we've wrestled with them. But in the midst of legitimate uncertainty about the Bible, we have discovered it to be a dazzling oasis of beauty and wisdom. We are grateful for our experiences and history with the Bible, but we recognize that many young people with the same experiences and histories walk away from the Bible and never look back. What we want to know is why. Why have so many millennials raised within Christianity turned away from viewing the Bible as authoritative and necessary? And recognizing that this is the case, what appeal can be made to our generation to invite them to reconsider the Bible?

I (Lauren) have felt the pull at various stages of my life to either be engaged with the Bible or ignore it. When I was young, it was easy to believe the Bible for what it claims to be—God's Word. But as I got older, I had my doubts. As a high school student, I sometimes felt that following the Bible meant living a life that was less fun for a life that was moral. Was that what I wanted? Then as I entered my twenties and faced greater hardships, I had to wonder whether God really cared. Why would he let me and those I loved experience the heartbreak of broken trust, caused by someone closest to me? Or why would the God of the Bible allow some of my deepest longings to go unfulfilled? When I moved out of my parents' home, I found that many people were willing to challenge the assumptions I had held—from professors to colleagues who were textual critics who cast doubt on the Bible's validity.

I remember, one day at work, leading a meeting with a number of brilliant scholars we had partnered with. Four of them had traveled to our office, while a few more were joining from various countries via videoconference. The group was meeting to discuss different aspects of research projects concerning biblical texts that were going on around the world, and my team was helping to manage logistics for these projects.

I was in my midtwenties, and I recall looking around the room and realizing that each of these colleagues had a PhD and spoke multiple languages and that many of them knew the languages that the biblical texts were written in. I was exposed to conversations and questions about the Bible's history and narrative that I had never encountered before. Seeing new, complex, and even difficult facets of a Book I had known my whole life created questions about the Bible I hadn't considered before. Believing in the Bible was no longer as easy as naively agreeing with whatever my trustworthy authority figures—mainly my parents and Sunday school teachers—were telling me.

Maybe you've also felt the Bible's foundations shaking beneath you, or maybe you've never found yourself truly Bible engaged to begin with. While my doubts were centered on the text that I had been engaged with for years, many millennials come to their doubts from a different perspective.

Among the Bible-open and Bible-closed, we have found some common objections to engaging with the Bible and believing it matters. These objections typically fall into two categories: cultural perception and personal experiences. Many people are wary of engaging with the Bible because they feel the culture at large has a negative perception of it; the Bible is viewed as being intolerant, outdated, and out of step with American cultural norms. To read the Bible or to live your life by it would mean pitting yourself against culture and isolating yourself from the mainstream.

Others are hesitant to engage with the Bible because their experiences with religion have been less than stellar. They grew up in a religious household or in the Bible Belt, and because of something a parent, a pastor, or a community said or did, they want nothing to do with the source of that old-time religion, the Bible.

It was with these questions and objections in mind that we felt led to write *Not What You Think*. This book is divided into four sections and twelve chapters. In the first section, we want to look at who we millennials are. In chapter 2, we will focus on the traits that characterize our generation—the good, the bad, and the misunderstood. In chapter 3, we will set the stage for the conversation by looking at our generation's struggle with defining truth and at the Bible's claim that it is truth, which together create a collision between millennials and the Bible. And in chapter 4, we will see how to view both the story of the Bible and our connection with this story. It is in this section that we look at what makes our generation unique and why that matters for understanding the Bible.

Part 2 is devoted to tackling the problem of cultural perception; this section is called "Where We Are From: The Bible and History." In chapter 5, having defined millennials, we now want to look at our history, how our views of and engagement with the Bible differ from those of past generations. Chapters 6 and 7 are focused on the impact that the Bible has had on culture and what makes its impact unique.

In part 3, we focus on personal experience. This is the millennial mind on the Bible. In chapter 8, we look at the importance of reading in general and find great encouragement in the reading habits of our fellow millennials. Chapters 9 and 10 delve into the personal nature of the story and message of the Bible and its impact on our spiritual development.

Finally, part 4 provides suggestions on how to begin a journey of Bible engagement. Chapter 11 answers the question, How do we read the Bible? Then we end with chapter 12, which issues a challenge to our generation. In our experience, we have found that if we millennials are who we claim we are, then we will be open-minded in this exploration of the most influential book of all time.

As millennials, we are all about clarity and transparency. We (Michael and Lauren) are not gurus, elite academics, or pundits. We are simply trying to ask questions, seek answers, and spur conversation. So here are some clarifications about what this book is and what it is not, which we hope will help you as you consider whether to continue with us on our journey of discovery.

WHAT THIS BOOK IS

- This book is an honest attempt by two millennials to tackle a controversial issue with sensitivity and kindness.
- This is a book written by two millennials for millennials and our generation Z siblings and those interested in knowing our generation and its relationship with the Bible.
- This book assesses where our generation is in reference to the Bible, and how we are similar to and different from previous generations.
- We hope to commend the Bible to millennials and gen Z and to challenge our generation to put its skepticism aside and give the Bible an opportunity to stand under scrutiny.

WHAT THIS BOOK IS NOT

- This book is not a how-to guide for reading the Bible, though we offer some helpful starting points and guides throughout the book. There are better books on that topic, and at the end of this book you will find a few listed. While reading books about the Bible is a *good* use of time, reading the Bible is a *great* use of time. We hope that no one neglects reading the Bible for the sake of visiting other people's thoughts on the Bible. Instead spend some quality time with the Good Book yourself!

- This is not a cross-generational rant about millennials. We are you! We are part of this generation. YouTube is full of TED talks and Facebook is covered with posts of interviews and lectures by members of other generations critical of millennials and our future. Unlike many, we have great hope for our generation, excitement about our potential, and confidence in the work we are already doing.

- Finally, this book is not an answer to all your questions about the Bible or a rebuttal to every argument you have ever heard that might cause you to be skeptical about the Bible. Rather this book is a challenge to you to have the kind of open mind that our generation is known for and to apply that mind to investigating the Bible's claims.

CHAPTER 2

WHAT IS A MILLENNIAL? THE FIVE I'S

This is your life. Are you who you want to be?

—JON FOREMAN, SWITCHFOOT

Gene Kranz was in turmoil. He stood in a room filled with rows of sophisticated computer consoles, operated by a group of the nation's most brilliant minds, and was sweating bullets over the possibility of losing three astronauts during the Apollo 13 mission. Kranz oversaw NASA's mission control center in Houston, Texas. After four days of pressure, an amazing feat of human ingenuity and massive computing power brought those three crewmen home alive. You know what's even more amazing? You have more computing power in your pocket than Kranz had in his mission control room. Technology has advanced so quickly in our lifetime that it has impacted many aspects of the millennial generation.

No technology in the past five centuries has shaped our world more than the internet. We (Michael and Lauren) have experienced two generation-defining moments that shaped our conception of who we are, as millennials, in this culture. Both of them centered on the internet, and both occurred in college. The first was purchasing our first iPhones. These small, sleek, simple, and powerful devices opened up a world of connectivity. The iPhone changed the way we communicated with each other as a dating couple in college and the way we related to the wider world around us.

The second generation-defining moment was when we received our college email accounts, for then we could finally register for an account on Facebook. Although we had been active on Xanga and had given Myspace a chance, Facebook was the long-awaited social media platform that was available only to college students. Being accepted into our university of choice was a plus, but logging on to *Facebook.com* for the first time was a thrill.

These moments changed us. We can no longer imagine our lives apart from our smartphones or social media. We suspect many of you would agree. They also represent two keys to understanding our generation. We have a relationship to technology unmatched by that of other generations, and a level of connectivity to people that previous generations could only have imagined. We are connected to the internet, yes, but it is more than that: we are connected to *each other*. As a result, we see others and the world differently than do our parents.

While these moments help define us in the minds of advertisers and pundits, they are hardly sufficient to define the experience of coming of age in the technology boom. If you asked one thousand young adults to share their most vivid childhood memories, you likely would get a range of answers, from the serious to the ridiculous—everything from Y2K to the election of the first African American president, from 9/11 to keeping up with the Kardashian family. One of the complexities of writing about any generation is that the best an author can do is to provide an explanation and theory about a snapshot in time. You attempt to capture a moment in a lifetime full of transition. The millennial generation is particularly difficult to pin down. Not only are we the most diverse generation in history, but the life stage we are now at is *marked* by transition and change.

In this chapter, we explore our generation—what makes us tick, what moves us, what marks us. We will look at five distinctives of our generation, each offering a piece of the mosaic that gives us an accurate image of millennials.

THIS IS US

In many ways, we (Michael and Lauren) are typical millennials; in other ways, we are complete outliers. We feel right at home in our generation, yet there are times when we feel out of place in our generation. We live for brunch, but we never went through a Chaco phase. We binge Netflix shows but have never used Tinder. We have made our pilgrimage to Harry Potter World, but we have never attended a music festival. We were all in on Pokémon, but we are out on poke.

This tension is emblematic of our generation and our stage in life. Demographically speaking, we are both just breaking into our thirties. So like all millennials, we were born roughly between 1980 and 2000. We are digital natives. Our earliest memories involve interacting with technology, and we can scarcely remember a time without internet access in our home. We share memories of key events with our friends and contemporaries; we experienced the bombing of the Murrah Building in Oklahoma City, 9/11, the War on Terror, and the Great Recession. We grew up alongside Harry, Ron, and Hermione. We watched Michael Phelps make Olympic history. And we witnessed the birth of social media. I (Michael) attended a public high school, and we both attended a public university.

So we definitely relate to our generation. Yet there are ways that we are different. Lauren and I are married, while 59 percent of the people in our generation are not.[1] We were married earlier than most in our generation, at age twenty-one, while the average age to be married in the US is twenty-six.[2] We live on our own, apart from any parental support. We have had stable, engaging employment throughout our marriage, while 71 percent of millennials report feeling disengaged at their jobs.[3] Then there is the Bible: we fall into the minority within the millennial generation in terms of what we think about and how we interact with the Bible. We are among the 9 percent of millennials who read the Bible daily and among the 30 percent who believe that the Bible is the inspired and inerrant Word of God.[4]

One aspect of our generation that we adore is the way millennials often defy stereotypes. We are not alone in feeling this tension of wanting to fit in yet not fitting the mold. As we have traveled and heard the experiences of so many young adults, we have found again and again that no one fits exactly into a narrow millennial stereotype. And given the largely negative perceptions others have of millennials, it's no wonder few of our peers want to be classified as part of our generation. It can be a death wish in terms of career advancement. One thing is for certain: the self-image and the self-definition of the millennial generation frequently differ from the image portrayed by critics and by culture in general.

In the same way that millennials have been misperceived by culture and pundits, the Bible has often been misrepresented by critics and culture. The Bible is too often judged by people who have not read it. We often meet people who have a negative view of millennials but have never had a relationship with one. We believe their whole concept would shift if they took the time to get to know a millennial. Perhaps the same could be said for the Bible. Might engaging with the Book change a person's understanding? If nothing else, it would likely change the stereotype someone might have of this Book and the people who read it.

As millennials, we often have had to combat the stereotypes associated with our generation. In 2012, the Boston Consulting Group, a marketing research firm, conducted a study of four thousand millennials and asked them to provide the word(s) that best described themselves and their generation. The top words millennials used to describe their generation included tech-savvy, hip, cool, young, innovative, and lazy. When compared to the responses of non-millennials describing millennials, you can easily see the contrast.[5] Non-millennials used words like lazy, entitled, spoiled, selfish, young, and tech-savvy.

There has been no shortage of attempts by sociologists, writers, pollsters, and pastors to define millennials. In true millennial style, we want to give you a glimpse of what we see and how we define our experience. We have identified five characteristics that mark our generation. They are by no means comprehensive, but we hope that exploring these characteristics will help get us all on the same page as we discuss how our generation interacts with the Bible. We call these traits the Five I's: immense, informed, impatient, impassioned, and integrated. (Michael is a preacher, so you will have to forgive him. Alliteration is in his blood; he can't help it.) Some of these are anecdotal, based on our experience, and some are based on research.

IMMENSE

Most of us grew up with parents who were baby boomers, a generation born immediately following World War II, from 1946 to 1964. Until our generation, the boomers were the largest generation in American history, about 75 million in total. Such large numbers created a tidal wave within the culture, shaping the moral, political, and economic landscape of America in a way no previous generation ever had. Their shared experience was marked by the arrival of the birth control pill, the Summer of Love, the Vietnam War, and Watergate. By 1980, though, a new wave had begun to form, and between 1980 and 2000 the number of annual live births in the US started to climb, from less than 3.5 million in the 1970s to 3.6 million, rising to an unprecedented 4 million live births a year between 1989 and 2000.[6] This produced the largest generation on record, the millennials, measuring at some 78 million strong.[7] By 2020, according to a Brookings Institution analysis, one in three adults will be a millennial, and by 2025 we will compose 75 percent of the US workforce.[8]

The relative size of our generation has affected the way in which we live and see ourselves. Belonging to such a large group can make us feel like we are part of something bigger than ourselves. Our generation is so big that we know we can effect change if we can rally and be heard. Because of this, millennials are often ready to speak up about issues we care about. On the flip side, being part of such a large group can mean getting lost in the noise. Millennials may be idealistic about effecting change because of our sheer numbers, yet many have also felt disillusioned by the thought that their voice may never be heard among such a crowded generation.

On the outside looking in, businesses and marketers have focused on us as a consumer base ever since we were children; entire advertising campaigns and hosts of products have been designed to appeal to our generation. This has created the sense among us that there is something special about our experience, regardless of whether this is true. It has also created a system in which millennials gravitate toward whatever the collective is interested in. While the Bible has been less and less of interest to our generation, the immensity and connection to each other can create an echo chamber in which new (or in this case, ancient) ideas are rarely heard. If marketers have filled our interests with the latest and greatest they have to offer us, there is little chance for a book to catch our interest. But what if this Book, the Bible, has more to offer us in true satisfaction than anything else our generation is chasing after?

Though the outcome of being part of a large generation is mixed, there is certainly a collective confidence that comes from knowing you are part of a monolithic, culture-altering group. However, when the loudest voices declare the Bible to be little more than a fairy tale, we can fall victim to groupthink before considering its claims for ourselves, out of fear of being shamed. For this reason, it's vital that we educate ourselves about this Book. Millennials are immense, but they are also informed.

INFORMED

Now, we must be careful here, because we can imagine that some of you, especially if you are not a millennial, may be thinking, *Oh great, another couple of millennials who think they know everything.* Definitely not what we mean! Instead, when we describe our generation as being informed, we mean that millennials came of age and entered the prime education stages of our lives—high school and college—in conjunction with the dawn of the information age. We are digital natives; by and large, we do not remember a time before the internet, personal computers, and smartphones. We are more at home than our non-millennial counterparts in accessing digital information and adopting new digital trends.[9] Sixty percent of millennials seek out news and analysis online; we are less likely than previous generations to get this from broadcast and print media.[10]

According to the American Press Institute, "The world is now literally in the pockets of the vast majority of Millennials much of the day. Fully 94 percent of those surveyed own smartphones connected to the internet. That compares with 69 percent of adults of all ages in their Personal News Cycle survey a year earlier."[11] We've got all the information we would ever need, on any topic, at the swipe of a finger.

Millennials also differ from other generations in terms of where we get other information. We are far less likely to trust official sources and corporations and far more likely to seek and trust information from our friends. "For this generation, the definition of 'expert'—a person with the credibility to recommend brands, products, and services—has shifted from someone with professional or academic credentials to potentially anyone with firsthand experience, ideally a peer or close friend."[12] We have a tendency to crowdsource our information, and the larger the crowd, the more likely we are to trust the information we receive. And since millennials are the largest generation, we are predisposed to trust each other more than outside sources. "U.S. Millennials also tend to seek multiple sources of information, especially from non-corporate channels, and they're likely to consult their friends before making purchase decisions."[13] Our generation's distrust of formal sources of information will be relevant in the next chapter as we consider millennials' relationship to the concept of truth.

Not only do we want information; we want it fast. This impatience gives us an edge when it comes to gathering data, but it can make us fall victim to the new at the expense of the tried and true. While the Bible is significant because it is old, we assume it to be outdated before reading the Book ourselves. We need to become informed about this Book, even if it takes us some time. Which leads us to the next trait of the millennial generation: we are impatient.

IMPATIENT

We (Michael and Lauren) used to live in New York City. We lived there from 2015 to 2016 because our work with Museum of the Bible was constantly taking us to the Northeast. We loved our tiny one-bedroom apartment tucked away in a quiet corner on the Upper West Side. While living there, we quickly discovered that everything takes longer in this city, from waiting for the subway to waiting in the longer-than-normal lines at restaurants. Just before we moved to New York City, we learned that Chick-fil-A—which is everywhere in our hometown—was opening its first location there. It was perfect. We knew we could survive living in the Big Apple as long as we had the comfort of those chicken nuggets and waffle fries. And of course the sauce. Yum! But what we found was that the weekly trip to Chick-fil-A was not the same as in the Midwest. When we were missing home and needed some sweet tea, we wanted it *now*. But the line in New York City was much longer than in Oklahoma City. The line was so long in the Manhattan location that it was often out the door. It tested our patience, but once we tasted that delicious, warm chocolate chip cookie after our meal, it was always worth it.

The two of us standing in line, learning to be patient while we waited for our favorite fast food, is a microcosm of what the millennial generation seems to be going through on a grander scale. One of the ways our technological age has affected our lives is that so much information has been made accessible so simply and with such amazing speed. We no longer need to go to a library to research some topic; we need only lift our smartphones. Even then, we don't need to type our request; we can simply speak to our digital friends Siri, Alexa, and Google.

We are used to fast access, fast food, and faster advancement. According to the Boston Consulting Group, millennials "are all about instant gratification. They put a premium on speed, ease, efficiency, and convenience in all their transactions. . . . Their preference for efficiency is even reflected in how they participate in causes."[14] Even in our generosity, we want instant results; among the 34 percent of millennials who make direct donations, we are three times more likely to do so on our mobile devices than non-millennials.

This efficiency with which we navigate the technological world has created in us a certain amount of intolerance for any institution or apparatus that slows down our progress. There is an inherent impatience among millennials for anything that smacks of inefficiency. Morgan Housel, a writer for the *Wall Street Journal*, makes this important point: "Impatience is the unwillingness to wait when there is no alternative to waiting. No tolerance for inefficiency is the unwillingness to wait when there is, or should be, a better alternative. The problem is that everyone knows impatience is basically a sin, right up there with greed and envy. But having no tolerance for inefficiency is the spark that has pushed every great innovation forward."[15]

So whether you see this impatience as a virtue or a vice depends largely on your point of view. In any case, if you see the Bible as a self-help book, you'll be disappointed that you are not growing from simply reading it. The Bible was not written to teach you a shortcut for upgrading your life. If you look to the Bible for a quick turnaround, you will find that your drive to succeed will leave you frustrated. We (Michael and Lauren) have come to have an empathetic, understanding view of our generation's impatience; we see it as a spark of passion and motivation. Which leads us to the fourth I: impassioned.

IMPASSIONED

Both of us have earned master's degrees from a seminary and are pursuing our PhDs. One of the reasons we are continuing on this prolonged course of education is because we both have a passion for religion, theology, and Christianity in particular. This mutual passion drives us to learn more, work harder, and integrate every part of our lives, both professionally and personally, with elements that fuel our passion. One of the distinctive marks of millennials is our passion, and we want to integrate every area of our lives with activities that feed it.

G. K. Chesterton, an English Christian who died in 1936, once offered some insight that neatly describes the passion motivating our generation: "The true soldier fights not because he hates what is in front of him, but because he loves what is behind him." This quote struck us because there is an underlying passion that drives us toward something more than serving our self-interest and getting rich. In their book *The Millennials: Connecting to America's Largest Generation*, Thom and Jess Rainer write, "Nine out of ten Millennials believe it is their responsibility to make a difference in the world. Millennials understand ownership. We are not depending on those generations that preceded us or those generations that will follow to do what needs to be done. . . . In addition to Millennials believing it is their responsibility to make a difference in the world, six out of ten Millennials believe they will make some great contribution in their lifetime. We believe the world is at our fingertips. Parents have instilled in us a belief that we can do anything. . . . We not only have the belief that we can make a difference; we have the desire to do so."[16]

Whereas previous generations created spaces apart from

their work and home life for advocacy and charity, we millennials are far more inclined to integrate our interests and passions into every area of our lives. The Boston Consulting Group and the Nielsen Company reveal this in their research on millennials.

The generation that was taught to recycle in kindergarten wants to be good to the planet and believes that collective action can make a difference. Millennials believe that working for causes is an integral part of life, and they are drawn to big issues. Instead of making one-off charitable donations in cash or in kind, they're more likely to integrate their causes into daily life by buying products that support sustainable farming or fair trade principles, or by joining large movements that aim to solve social or environmental problems.[17]

Three-quarters of Millennials made a financial gift to a non-profit in 2011, but the gifts were within their means, typically less than $100. Even though they can't make large donations, they contribute to their causes in other ways, with 71 percent raising money on behalf of a non-profit, and 57 percent . . . doing volunteer work in the past year—more than any other generation.[18]

It is not enough for us to have a job; we want a job that allows us to pursue the causes we believe in. "Sixty-four percent of Millennials would rather make $40,000/year at a job they love than $100,000/year at a job they think is boring" or does not allow them to pursue their beliefs.[19] "Millennials are more likely than their older counterparts to indicate that they're willing to spend more for goods and services from companies that have implemented programs to give back to society, and this willingness to spend more has risen over the past two years. Over 60 percent are also willing to pay more for a product if it's good for the environment."[20] It is also not enough that we have a hobby or make a purchase or eat a meal; we want our time and our dollars to make a difference. We want that hobby to be fun but also eco-friendly; we want our purchase of TOMS shoes to mean that a child living in poverty can have a pair of shoes; we want to enjoy a meal knowing that no one was exploited for their labor.

We love this about our generation, and we applaud and defend this passion. Our capacity for passion is no accident of culture or society. It is not a random twist of fate or demographics that we are part of such an impassioned generation. The capacity to care, and the drive to translate that care into action, is emblematic of a larger desire in each of us, which we will talk more about later.

Millennials are immense, we are informed, we are impatient, and we are impassioned; each of these traits speaks to a unique part of our generational experience. But we have reserved the final I—integrated—for last, for a reason. Because out of all the markers of our generation, our desire for and experience of social connectedness is perhaps the most defining feature.

INTEGRATED

What do we mean when we speak of being integrated? To us, integration is more than taking two halves and making a whole; it's combining two wholes so they become inseparable. We believe this is true of our generation in two fundamental ways: individually, millennials are integrated with technology in ways previous generations never have been; collectively, millennials are experiencing a new level of social integration. Our integration with one another is happening *through* our integration with technology. Both types of integration work together in concert to produce a level of social engagement and connectivity that previous generations scarcely could imagine. Technology allows us to connect socially, and we are literally connected to our technology, so the result is that we are in constant social connection. Nielsen, the ratings agency and media trends company, helps us understand to what extent: "Millennials are glued to their smartphones, making mobile an efficient way to reach them. An astounding 83 percent say that they sleep with their smartphones, compared with 50 percent of Boomers."[21] And nearly 100 percent of millennials own a cell phone.[22]

This constant contact with technology allows us to connect to one another socially, which we are far more prone to do than are older generations. Nielsen makes this important point in its 2014 study: "[Millennials] started the social networking movement from their dorm rooms. In a survey asking Millennials who they believe defines their generation, Mark Zuckerberg, founder of Facebook, topped the charts. As sharers, Facebook is a platform for 72 percent of Millennials. Millennials are an open book, sharing all their thoughts, pictures and videos instantly with their online community—20 percent update their Facebook status multiple times per day, while 36 percent of Boomers report never updating their status. Compared with Boomers, they aren't as concerned with privacy and security issues in sharing personal information online."[23]

We share our lives, our meals, our relationships, and our

hearts with the watching world. But this blurring of the public and private spheres has its downside: we can be relaxing after a long day, sitting on the couch, and be connected to our friends half a world away on Facebook but disconnected to each other in the same room. Many times, we (Michael and Lauren) have looked up from our phones only to realize that we spent the past hour connecting to everyone in our lives but each other. This is a shadow cast by all modern social connection. As a generation, we are often integrated but rarely intimate.

There is no end to our generation's hunger for social interaction. We crave a socially integrated life, but the experience of that life through social media rarely leaves us satisfied. This desire, more than any other trait we millennials possess, points to a deeper longing we all have to be known and to experience intimacy with someone else. This desire is natural; it is part of who we were created to be. The question is, If we cannot get what we need from our social networks, doesn't this point to the reality that we were created for something more than what social networks can provide? We'll discover that this *something* that our generation is searching for is found in the Bible.

Our effort to define our generation is not comprehensive. Yet these traits have resonated with us personally, and we have observed them in our friends and family. We hope that these traits resonate with you, but even if they don't all connect with your experience, we invite you to walk with us as we discover how this complex and multifaceted group relates to the Bible and what it might look like for them to (re)engage with the Bible.

So as we hold up a mirror to millennials, we find a generation that is:

- *Immense.* At 78 million, we are the largest generation living. This has created the sense among our generation that there is something special about our experience, regardless of whether this is true. There is also a collective confidence that comes from knowing we are part of a monolithic, culture-altering group.
- *Informed.* We are more at home than our non-millennial counterparts in accessing digital information and adopting new digital trends.[24] Sixty percent of millennials seek out news and analysis online, though we are less likely than previous generations to seek information from broadcast and print media.
- *Impatient.* We want it all right now. Technology has created in us a certain amount of intolerance for any institution or apparatus that slows down our progress. There is an inherent impatience among millennials for anything that smacks of inefficiency.
- *Impassioned.* One of the things that makes millennials distinct is our passion, and we want to integrate every facet of our lives with activities that feed this passion.
- *Integrated.* As a generation, we are experiencing a new level of social integration. Not only are we integrated socially; our connection to one another happens seamlessly through our connection to technology. Yet as a generation, we are often integrated but rarely intimate.

Millennials are a generation poised for influence. And to optimize this influence, we first must wrestle openly and honestly with the nature of truth.

CHAPTER 3

OUR PROBLEM WITH TRUTH

Truth does not change according to
our ability to stomach it.

—FLANNERY O'CONNOR

The great enemy of the truth is very often not the
lie—deliberate, contrived, and dishonest—but the
myth—persistent, persuasive, and unrealistic.

—JOHN F. KENNEDY

On a warm September night during our sophomore year at the University of Oklahoma, Michael and I went on a unique date. We walked that evening across campus and arrived at Meachum Auditorium at 7:00 p.m., took our seats in the balcony, and waited for the speaker. We were both enrolled in a class called Religion, Culture, and the Meaning of Life, and for extra credit, we were attending a lecture by the author and professor Bart Ehrman. Although our date lacked traditional romance, it was an evening that neither of us would ever forget.

Ehrman is a professor at the University of North Carolina at Chapel Hill. He was on the lecture circuit for his book *Misquoting Jesus*, which had recently released. His book provides an overview of the changes found in the surviving copies of the New Testament and of the scribes who produced them. Ehrman has made a name for himself as someone who grew up a Christian and attended the evangelical Wheaton College but left Christianity in graduate school.

He opened the evening with a story, describing an instance in his class in which he polled the 360 students there by asking them a few questions. He first asked how many of the students believed that the Bible was the Word of God. A large number of hands shot up. He then asked how many had read *The Da Vinci Code* by Dan Brown (you can tell this was some years ago). Again the majority raised their hands. His final question was where it got interesting. He asked how many of them had read the Bible. Only a few students raised their hands.

Ehrman offered this inference: something was clearly wrong if a majority of the room affirmed that the Bible was the Word of God even though very few had actually read it, whereas Dan Brown's fictional story about symbols and saints had been devoured cover to cover.

There was an obvious disconnect between what people believed and how people acted. Ehrman used this disconnect as the basis for his criticisms of evangelicals and their devotion to the Book that, apparently, many were unfamiliar with. Throughout the rest of the lecture, Ehrman presented well-crafted criticism of the very text that we, and many others in the room, had claimed to base our lives on. He cast doubt on the reliability of the text itself, because of errors that took place in the translation and transmission process. He explained, with great detail and academic authority, that we simply could not trust the text of the Bible. No two copies of the New Testament were exactly alike, so how were we to know what the Bible actually said?

Michael and I were both Christians, and we sat in the auditorium feeling very much out of place. As we listened to Ehrman's lecture, we grew frustrated at having our faith and our concept of truth challenged in a way that we had not previously experienced. Walking out of the room afterward with our classmates, we heard the conversations around us and noticed how readily members of our generation accepted Ehrman's critiques and were willing to turn their backs on the Bible's claims of truth.

Ehrman did not completely discount the Bible per se or those who believe in it; rather he built a case against taking the Bible's claims seriously, on the contention that we do not know what the original authors of the Bible wrote. We don't have the original writings or complete early copies of the Bible. Therefore, just as we cannot trust the final message in a game of telephone, we cannot trust the copies we have of the Bible. The Bible may still be an interesting book, but if we can't know what the original writing said because of the errors between manuscripts, then we are unable to know what this Book actually taught. To the hundreds of millennial students listening to Ehrman that night, his argument seemed perfectly normal. The message was loud and clear: objective truth is unknowable; ultimately, it comes down to your interpretation; ultimately, it comes down to you and what you think.

Every year, the *Oxford English Dictionary (OED)* names its word of the year. This choice is based on the word's frequency of use during the year and whether the word summarizes the general cultural moment. In 2016, *OED*'s word was *post-truth*, defined as "relating to or denoting circumstances in which objective facts are less influential in shaping public opinion than appeals to emotion and personal belief." Our era is one in which truth has moved from objective reality to personal response. Our generation generally hesitates to accept any truth outside of personal experience and opinion. We like to avoid arguments about personal behavior, morals, politics, and religion by employing the well-worn phrase "Well, whatever works for you; we all have our own truths." But rather than end conflicts, this kind of response seems to create a lack of authenticity by shutting out conversations about anyone's real convictions, and rather than foster clarity, this response creates confusion.

As we (Michael and Lauren) consider millennials and their views on truth, we see three things that would be helpful to address. First, we see a need for truth; second, we see a dissatisfaction with modern, secular substitutes for truth;

and third, we will see a solution offered by a popular spirituality misconception about truth, as well as a possible answer to the need and dissatisfaction millennials are facing.

THE NEED

What is truth? If my truth is different from your truth, is it really *true*? Whether we realize it or not, we long for truth. We see truthful people as good, and we make statements about reality. Truth is real, factual, sincere.

In a world where there is no truth, there is no justice. We benefit in the West from a stable justice system. We (Michael and Lauren) do not pretend it is perfect, but we have traveled outside of the United States enough to see justice systems where no citizen is safe and corruption cannot be challenged. When people appeal to a sense of right and wrong, they are assuming a common truth that should be accepted by society. Thieves are punished for stealing. Murderers are brought to justice for killing. Our sense of justice is based on an assumption of universal truth. And it reveals that deep down, we need truth.

Each and every one of us has this need for truth, despite what many in our culture believe and insist. We need a reality, provable facts, and consistent behavior to ground us. Our need for truth is not limited to one particular area of our lives; it affects us in every area as individuals and as a community.

Truth is objective, but we all approach it subjectively. We all begin forming our conception of truth with the most basic understanding of what is real and what is not real. This happens early in life, when our parents or caregivers teach us the fundamentals, like the difference between an apple and a chair.

When we wake up in the middle of the night after a bad dream, our parents explain to us the difference between reality and imagination. Our parents and other people we trust—teachers, mentors, even our peers—help us understand the difference between truth and fiction. Finally, we encounter the idea of truth as sincerity, or character. We begin to understand that there is a link between our experience with those around us and our interaction with the truth. Sincerity doesn't make something true, but we should be sincere about what we hold as truths. Because truth is reality.

We (Michael and Lauren) would like to suggest something that may seem counterintuitive—even countercultural—to our fellow millennials: Sometimes a new reality—an acceptance of a new truth—changes the way we live. In other cases, our accepted truths are affirmed and solidified by our experiences. Either way, truth must be dealt with. We know this is a bold statement, so let us explain.

We each came to realize that there are external truths that come into contact with our lives, whether we want to admit it or not. C. S. Lewis once wrote, "You never know how much you really believe anything until its truth or falsehood becomes a matter of life and death to you." This lesson took on even greater depth and meaning for me (Lauren) when I turned sixteen.

I had a newly minted driver's license, and I was loving the freedom that it brought me. My driver's education had taught me many important safety lessons, one of which had to do with a seat belt. I would be more likely to survive a car accident if the belt was properly fastened. I am glad I took this fact as truth.

One day, after having my license for only a few months, I was driving to my grandparents' house to deliver flowers to my grandma for her birthday. I was stopped at a stoplight on a quiet street when suddenly I heard screeching. I glanced up, and in my rearview mirror I saw a car headed straight for me. Time seemed to move in slow motion. There was nothing I could do to avoid the impact. Reflexively, I braced myself by putting my hands on the steering wheel and stomped on the brakes because there was another car stopped in front of me.

Then a loud crash. A car going at least 45 mph had slammed into me. I screamed. Glass shattered all around me. I heard the sound of fluid leaking, and all I could imagine was the movie scenes I had seen in which someone's car blew up because of a gas leak. I was terrified, so I quickly put the car in park, unbuckled, and got out. Thankfully, nothing was broken and nothing seemed to be bleeding. Praise God, the other driver and I were both relatively unharmed. With my first car totaled, I was grateful to walk away with nothing more than whiplash. The seat belt had held me back when I could have hit my face against the steering wheel, causing serious injury or worse. That experience early in my driving career taught me to value the fact—the truth—that wearing a seat belt increases safety and saves lives. This truth had proved significant in a very real life-or-death scenario in my life. This truth wasn't something I could throw around, telling my friends, "Seat belts may be true for you, but who are you to say they are my truth?" I had experienced the truth of seat belts for myself, and I was convinced!

At different times, Michael and I both came to the conclusion—and some of you probably have experienced this as well—that the truth may be deniable, but in the end it is immovable and unavoidable. Often, you come to terms with the truth when you have no other choice. The truth is like light. It illuminates and exposes what is real. This is why

Jesus claimed that if people followed him and his teachings, "then you will know the truth, and the truth will set you free" (John 8:32). We'll talk more about this later, but he offers the kind of freedom that comes from living and breathing what is true. Instinctively, we can appreciate this and recognize that we have a need for this kind of stability. And then there is this old Jewish proverb: "Buy the truth and do not sell it" (Prov. 23:23). Truth is that valuable! Our generation hungers for an answer and desires to find something valuable that we can believe in and trust. While we are an informed generation, linked together by technology, aware of many of the answers our culture provides, our instinctive hunger for truth continues, and we experience a gnawing dissatisfaction.

THE DISSATISFACTION

The need for truth and some basis for reality begins to seem unavoidable the more life we live. As we experience missed promotions we felt we deserved, false assurances from politicians, and injustices to our family, we start to recognize that there are truths that will impact our lives. So the question becomes, Where do we find the truth we seek? On the whole, as millennials, we seem far less likely than previous generations to turn to religion or other institutional sources for answers to questions about how to deal with the fog of relative truth in an ever-changing world, which the current exodus of millennials from the church illustrates. Not only are millennials walking away from religion, but we've seen friends choose to disassociate with the church. There is a reluctance to be a part of anything religious or institutional. The Gallup organization finds that "the percentage of

Americans who are eschewing religious affiliation also appears to be on the rise, with Millennials leading this trend. In 2008, 23% of this generation said they had no religious preference. By 2015, this number climbed 7 points. The older generations also saw a modest bump in those claiming no religious preference, but no more than 1 to 2 points each."[1]

More than any other generation, millennials are seeking their answers elsewhere. One of the hallmarks of our informed and technologically integrated generation is our tendency to turn toward one another when seeking answers, advice, and perspectives on the truth. The Boston Consulting Group (BCG) found that this phrase was common among millennials: "I trust my friends more than 'corporate mouthpieces.'"[2] BCG continues:

> For this generation, the definition of "expert"—a person with the credibility to recommend brands, products, and services—has shifted from someone with professional or academic credentials to potentially anyone with firsthand experience, ideally a peer or close friend. U.S. Millennials also tend to seek multiple sources of information, especially from noncorporate channels, and they're likely to consult their friends before making purchase decisions. For example, more Millennials than non-Millennials reported using a mobile device to read user reviews and to research products while shopping (50 percent versus 21 percent). "Crowd sourcing"—tapping into the collective intelligence of the public or one's peer group—has become particularly popular. The reach and accessibility of social media have amplified the voices of individual consumers. Now anyone can become an expert. Messages that resonate are quickly

spread and reinforced through user reviews and other online forums.[3]

In a way, we have turned from objective sources of truth to a kind of crowdsourcing of truth. I (Lauren) have noticed this in my life. If I want to know where the best brunch spot is in a city, I don't care about advertisements; I want to see what the reviews are saying. A few weekends ago, Michael and I were in a new city for a retreat, and we had time for one brunch meal. As always, I started googling "best brunch spots" and looking at the reviews. I pulled up Yelp and saw what others were saying. I also looked at the photos people had posted, because aesthetics and presentation matter. If I see an ad come up on Instagram for a brunch spot, I am not likely to trust it. I am way more likely to want to try a spot if my friends are raving about it. Eggs Benedict or chicken and waffles—this is a serious decision, right?

I do this in other areas of my life too. I want to know what my friends think about where to shop for groceries, what to consider when buying a home, or what doctor to see. This is common among millennials. While the Boston Consulting Group was addressing our tendency to seek the wisdom of our peers when making market decisions, an argument can be made that we also do this with even larger life choices, such as whether to believe in God and what values and morals to live by. Our community affects substantially more than just our breakfast choices.

We would like to suggest a possible problem with this consensus approach to truth: How can we be sure that the input we are getting is true or even helpful? What if the consensus on a life choice goes against our opinion or is potentially harmful? How do we determine how to live our lives? While we absolutely believe in the importance of community and allowing others to speak into our lives, we think there are other factors that can help speak into these deeper questions about God, morals, and life.

This is where the idea of worldview is crucial. A worldview is simply the way you view the world. It's the set of concepts that influence how you interact with the world. Almost like a pair of sunglasses or fashion glasses, coloring how you see the world and your culture. We all have one. You may be conscious of your worldview, but most likely you act out of your worldview every day without knowing it. This is why worldview is so hard to define and so hard to challenge; we often are unaware of how our worldview impacts us. Consider what American sociologist James Davison Hunter suggests: "'Worldview' is so deeply embedded in our consciousness, in the habits of our lives, and in our social practices that to question one's worldview is to question 'reality' itself. . . . This is why one cannot merely change worldviews or question one's own very easily. Most of what really counts, in terms of what shapes us and directs us, we are not aware of; it operates far below what most of us are capable of consciously grasping."[4]

The worldview of every religion—Christianity included—is rooted in an objective reality that is framed by a text as well as the consistent interpretation of that text. So when disputes arise, when disagreements occur, one can easily return to the source, asking the question, What does the text say? Christians would ask, What does the Bible say? We recognize that this sounds simplistic, yet it is the starting point for discovering the Christian reality. But within cultural consensus, within the crowd of our peers, how can we know what worldview we are dealing with?

A COMMON WAY TO VIEW THE WORLD

The most common worldview that we've noticed in our culture today, even among many Christians, is something called moralistic therapeutic deism (MTD), or simply the view that God is distant and wants us to be good people so that we feel good about ourselves. Michael and I first came across this concept a few years ago in seminary. The terminology of MTD was developed by the sociologist Christian Smith at the University of Notre Dame. There are three important parts to the cultural phenomenon of moralistic therapeutic deism.

Moralistic

Millennials "believe that central to living a good and happy life is being a good, moral person. That means being nice, kind, pleasant, respectful, and responsible; working on self-improvement; taking care of one's heath; and doing one's best to be successful."[5] Few would disagree; almost all of us feel this way. We tend to see a correlation between happiness and morality, in which *morality* means being good to other people, obeying the "do no harm" principle. It is okay to live as we want, just as long as we are not infringing on the life or happiness of others. In many ways, you could call it millennial morality. It is, essentially, personal and isolated. The questions become, How do we define even our own morality? On what do we base our conclusion as to what is right and wrong? These questions trouble us, for no one is an island unto themselves; we all form our individual morality according to the various influences in our lives, and we all have different influences. These diverse influences often push us to different conclusions about what is right and what is wrong. The question we millennials should consider wrestling with is this: Is it possible to land on morality apart from an objective source?

Therapeutic

The word therapeutic can feel undefined or unclear. I (Michael) think of therapeutic as describing actions, words, or choices that feel positive or healing. Being moral is therapeutic; it feels good. So we strive for morality so we can be happy and find peace. Smith writes, "This is not a religion of repentance from sin, of keeping the Sabbath, of living as a servant of a sovereign divine, of steadfastly saying one's prayers, of faithfully observing high holy days, of building character through suffering, of basking in God's love and grace, of spending oneself in gratitude and love for the cause of social justice, etc. Rather, what appears to be the actual dominant religion among U.S. [millennials] is centrally about feeling good, happy, secure, at peace. It is about attaining subjective well-being, being able to resolve problems, and getting along amiably with other people."[6] There is no denying that millennials are motivated by feeling good. We like our safe spaces, and we do not like personal confrontation. While we are ready, willing, and able to advocate for what we believe in, we tend to avoid interpersonal confrontation. One reason why so many millennials are turned off to traditional religion stems from the habit and history of confrontation they have witnessed and even experienced in religious movements and denominations, particularly as these have interacted with culture.

Except here's the irony: millennials consistently express to us a general dissatisfaction with the pursuit of happiness and doing what feels good. Even finding meaning in one's career or studies does not guarantee peace in one's life. Despite millennials' dislike of confrontation, the anonymity of their social media feeds creates an environment of criticism and sometimes even bullying, making personal peace elusive. So here's something we wonder about: Is there a way to find happiness in some truth outside one's own experience?

Deism

Finally, if millennials deal with the God question at all, it is by embracing deism. What is deism? Although deism acknowledges the existence of God, as Smith writes, "this God is not Trinitarian, he did not speak through the Torah or the prophets of Israel, was never resurrected from the dead, and does not fill and transform people through his Spirit. This God is not demanding. He actually can't be, since his job is to solve our problems and make people feel good. In short, God is something like a Divine Butler and Cosmic Therapist—he is always on call, takes care of any problems that arise, professionally helps his people to feel better about themselves, and does not become too personally involved in the process."[7]

In the 2007 film *Evan Almighty*, Steve Carell plays a congressman named Evan, a modern-day Noah who has a wife named Joan and three sons. Evan prays to God—in this case, Morgan Freeman—asking the Almighty to give his family the opportunity to grow closer, to be happy, and to improve the environment. Soon afterward, strange events begin occurring in Evan's life. He has visions, he miraculously grows a beard, animals begin to follow him around, and he becomes convinced he is to build an ark, just like the one in the Bible.

Evan constructs his ark with God's guidance, his family's assistance, and several funny interactions with animals and the local government in Prestige Crest, Virginia. A flood occurs when a nearby dam breaks. Evan and his family are whisked off to safety, and his doubters are proved wrong. God appears and informs Evan that his prayer has been answered, his family is close again, the environment has been cleaned, and the world can be changed through acts of random kindness (ARK).

With a Rotten Tomatoes rating of 23 percent, this movie is probably not one you'll want to stream anytime soon. But it brilliantly displays Christian Smith's idea of moralistic therapeutic deism. Evan just wants to be happy and do well; he wants his family to be close and happy, and the environment to be clean and safe. God, while really cool and dressed in a boss white suit, is pretty powerless to effect any change. He allows Evan to embark on a journey during which Evan finds the strength to complete his act of random kindness and change the world and unite his family.

Unlike the story of Noah in the Bible, *Evan Almighty* features none of the biblical concepts of human rebellion against God or of judgment for our bad choices, there is no tension in the relationship between God and humanity, and there appears to be no need for rescuing humanity from its alienated, angsty condition. The entire Hollywood story—all the work to build the ark, and the eventual flood—is centered on one man and his family and their pursuit of peace, love, and togetherness. This is the essence of deism: God is present but powerless; he is reduced to a bystander who dispenses truth and rules and the occasional pearl of wisdom to those for whom happiness remains elusive.

In this equation, God is not a source of objective truth, only a rubber stamp on your version of whatever you believe truth to be, whatever you determine you need to do to move forward and accomplish your goals. What is surprising to us is the large number of Christians who seem to unconsciously subscribe to this belief. They claim that God exists and is powerful, but like the students in Bart Ehrman's classroom, they have little time in their lives for figuring out who God is or what he has to say. No wonder they do not find this deistic God compelling. But we do wonder: What if God was something more than a simple rubber stamp on your life? What if he wasn't distant and uncaring but intimately familiar with you and your struggles and invested in your joy? Would that change your opinion about him and his Word?

As we have sought truth and processed what truth means, we have asked ourselves whether the crowd and the culture satisfy. As we have at times crowdsourced truth, we have questioned whether we are finding comfort in the crowd. How about you?

We wonder whether those who object to religion and to Christianity in particular do so either because they have a false understanding of what Christianity is or because they have a difficult time accepting any truth that infringes on their crowdsourced concept of what will make them happy. So in turn they stereotype Christians and unthinkingly believe in systems which allow them to remain just as they want to be. What worries us is how easily we can be fooled into accepting as truth something we like to hear but in reality is harmful, while rejecting what sounds uncomfortable but is really for our good. The Danish philosopher Søren Kierkegaard said, "There are two ways to be fooled. One is to believe what isn't true; the other is to refuse to believe what is true." We hope that in this book, we can challenge you to contend with what might be true, even if it makes you uneasy and unsure because it upends your worldview.

Pursuing and struggling with truth is by no means unique to our generation. While we millennials may be unique in our time and in our culture, we can take some comfort in knowing we are wrestling with questions that have plagued individuals for thousands of years.

We began this chapter with a story of a man standing in front of a crowd, challenging the conception of truth, and we would like to end with a similar story. In the book of John, one of the books of the Bible that chronicles the events of Jesus' life, the apostle John shares the story of a man who stood before a crowd and didn't question truth; rather he claimed to *be* truth. Near the last day of his life, Jesus stood before a Roman governor named Pontius Pilate. Jesus had been arrested by the Jewish authorities and brought to Pilate for trial. The authorities were determined to have Jesus put to death for violating their religious rules and codes, so they insinuated that he was an enemy of Rome, opposing Caesar's taxes and claiming to be a king. Pilate was the one who could legally determine whether a prisoner would be sentenced to die or be set free. There was only one problem: Pilate could not find, in any testimony or any account, any record of Jesus having committed a crime worthy of death. Pilate, a Roman, was asked to judge a Jewish matter, something from an entirely different culture. Can you imagine this as a millennial nightmare—being called on to judge someone else according to their cultural background and personal claims? John picks up the story here.

Pilate then went back inside the palace, summoned Jesus and asked him, "Are you the king of the Jews?"

"Is that your own idea," Jesus asked, "or did others talk to you about me?"

"Am I a Jew?" Pilate replied. "Your own people and chief priests handed you over to me. What is it you have done?"

Jesus said, "My kingdom is not of this world. If it were, my servants would fight to prevent my arrest by the Jewish leaders. But now my kingdom is from another place."

"You are a king, then!" said Pilate.

Jesus answered, "You say that I am a king. In fact, the reason I was born and came into the world is to testify to the truth. Everyone on the side of truth listens to me."

"What is truth?" retorted Pilate. With this he went out again to the Jews gathered there and said, "I find no basis for a charge against him."

—John 18:33–38

What we see in this instance is a man, Pilate, struggling to come to terms with someone with a unique claim on truth. Pilate's struggle is our struggle; two thousand years later we are still trying to decide whether we can know the truth and whether the truth does in fact have a bearing on our lives. As we close this chapter and our discussion on truth, consider this: What if truth is not just a point of view? What if truth is not just a list of rules—yours, ours, or anyone else's? What if truth is not the ever-changing consensus of the crowd but instead is a person whom you get to know and who knows you? This person's story is told in the Bible. His name is Jesus, and in the next chapter, we will explore how every part of the Bible points to him.

CHAPTER 4

WHAT IS THE BIBLE'S MESSAGE?

If you believe what you like about the Gospel,
and reject what you don't like, it is not the
Gospel you believe in, but yourself.

—SAINT AUGUSTINE

A classic is a book that has never
finished saying what it has to say.

—ITALO CAVINO

An increasing number of people who grow up in the faith later reject that faith in adulthood. We and others refer to these individuals as nones—those who profess no religious affiliation whatsoever. You've likely met someone who had this story; they went to church when they were young but today are not religious. Familiarity does not always produce faith. Simply being exposed to faith or even reading the Bible is no guarantee of becoming a Christian.

Many people consider themselves religious but are disengaged from or apathetic toward the Bible; they have been exposed to the Bible, but they are not excited by it. Many would describe themselves as being repelled by the Bible and the religion it represents. According to Barna, 18 percent of Americans are skeptical toward the Bible, and within that 18 percent the single largest demographic is that of millennials, 26 percent of whom report feeling that way.[1] One in three millennials—the highest percentage (33 percent) of any age group surveyed—view the Bible as merely another book.[2]

In our conversations with college students and young people, we have noticed that the greatest confusion surrounding the Bible has to do with its message. Few seem to know what the message of the Bible actually is. Among our interactions with our generation on social media, there is confusion about what it means to live out the Bible's teachings. When we ask the question, What is the message of the Bible? we often receive one of three responses having to do with what the Bible *is*: it is a rule book, a source of inspiration, or a fairy tale.

A Rule Book. Some seem to view the Bible as a restrictive how-to guide. Often, these people have tried to apply the various laws and admonitions of the Bible to every facet of their life. The motivation for this obedience is to demonstrate moral superiority to others or to God based on their adherence to the rules. (This is often called legalism.) But viewing the Bible in such a legalistic way brought discouragement and ultimately left them disheartened, as they never seemed able to meet the standards of "living biblically." They also may have become turned off by the tendency of some others in their community to view the Bible as a political playbook. When the Bible becomes the property of one political party, the result is inevitably alienation and rejection.

A Source of Inspiration. This middle group is skeptical about the Bible not because they hate it, not because they don't trust it, not even because they don't think it is a religious text. No, this group's skepticism stems from their view of the Bible as merely a collection of inspirational stories and quotes. They find encouragement in some of the Bible's stories; they may even affirm a good generic biblical quotation from time to time. But when it comes to using the Bible as a guide for life, a way to define morality, a source of truth and ethics, they become hesitant. Unfortunately, there are a number of Christian preachers and televangelists who do little to discourage this view, and frequently quote verses or passages in the Bible to accommodate beliefs and therapies which have little to do with the core message of the Bible. The Bible's main message, as understood by many people of faith, is about trusting Jesus' death and resurrection to save us from sin and then living in response to his free gift of salvation. We won't understand the Bible's true message if we're simply picking and choosing inspirational verses because they make us feel good.

A Fairy Tale. Our final group of skeptics rejects the Bible because they were taught to regard it as merely a legend. Whether at home, high school, or college, the Bible was held to be nothing more than a piece of literature (think *The Lord of the Rings*, but in Hebrew and Greek). So any claims that the Bible might make on one's life, or any appeals to the Bible's authority in society or culture, would be the same as if it were George R. R. Martin's *Game of Thrones*. Atheist Richard Dawkins would be firmly in this camp. Dawkins, who is an ardent opponent of Christianity, has some appreciation for the Bible, but only as an influential work of literature. He states, "The good book should be read as a great work of literature—but it is not a guide to morality."[3]

The lesson from these three groups is this: when the message of the Bible is unclear to the reader, the meaning of the Bible is lost. If there is widespread disagreement about the Bible's message in our culture, then it should be no surprise when we assign little value to its meaning in our lives. So let's dig deeper into the all-important question, What is the message of the Bible?

THE RULES OF THE BOOK

Lauren loves Harry Potter. I do as well, but Lauren *truly* loves the series. She has read the books, and we both have binged on all eight films numerous times. Many a night, when we want to relax, we will pop some popcorn and turn on one of the movies.

I struggled a bit to get into the story line of Harry Potter, with its witches and wizards, flying broomsticks and magic wands. My instinct is to say, "Wait, that could never happen; there is no way a kid could fly like that." In a sense, though, when I raise such an objection, I am not being fair to the story. I have learned that one of the keys to enjoying and even benefiting from great works of literature is to enter the world of the text. That world may be different from the world we know, yet in order to be fair to the text, we have to accept the rules of that world. We need to approach a text on its own terms. If in the Harry Potter universe there are wizards who can cast spells and fly and change their appearance, then it would be unfair to judge Harry according to our universe, where none of those things are possible. Part of what allows the story to make sense and be entertaining is the understanding that Harry has to behave according to the rules of his story, not ours. Let Harry be Harry.

One of the most common objections to the Bible, with its record of miraculous and supernatural events, is that it cannot have any relevance to our modern, physical world. But part of understanding and appreciating the message of the Bible is accepting the rules of the text. As with Harry Potter, we need to let the Bible be the Bible. The Bible records a story of a supernatural God of immense power who exists before creation, and his interaction with that creation. He is both present in our time and timeless. He is both limited by his character and limitless in his ability to mold all of history to his purpose. He is both apart from the physical world and a part of the physical world in the presence of the man Jesus Christ.

When you come to the Bible and you see rules, laws, and prescriptions for living, it might be easy to react and say that those laws do not make sense or that the story is not relevant.

But remember, within the universe of the biblical story, those rules and laws make perfect sense. A Creator has a perfect right to prescribe the actions of what he has created; he has the same rights of ownership that any of us would have over something that we created.

When you feel the pull toward skepticism about the supernatural elements of the biblical story—worldwide floods, seas parting, people walking on water—try to enter into the story on the Bible's terms. Again, let the Bible be the Bible. In the Bible's universe, the supernatural is real and the very source of our natural reality.

In a relationship, there are always two sides to every conflict. To gain full perspective, you need to listen to the other person and put yourself in their shoes; you need to enter their rules of reality to understand. It would be unfair to judge a person based merely on what you know or have experienced. Likewise, to begin to grasp the message of the Bible, we have to accept the rules of its story and be open to its world and the perspective that it presents to us. In order for the Bible to begin to make sense, we need to let God be God.

THE SOURCE OF INSPIRATION

Both Michael and I have struggled over the years to make sense of the Bible's message. Honestly, the church culture that we grew up in did not make it easy. We would read or have read to us stories from the Bible, like David and Goliath or Sampson and Delilah, but rarely did the stories ever seem to connect. Like so many who have casually engaged with the Bible, you catch a story here and a story there, maybe see a movie like

The Ten Commandments, *Noah*, *Exodus*, or the Jesus film, and something seems to be missing; they all seem disconnected, with no overarching plot. Growing up, we often thought that while these stories in and of themselves were inspirational and encouraging, there had to be some connection between them other than that they all came from the Bible.

When we were in high school, a new preacher came to our church. Rick Thompson began teaching through different books of the Bible. He taught many of the same familiar stories, yet he had a different perspective that helped bring these disjointed tales into view as one overarching narrative that flows from creation to fall, redemption, and restoration. Pastor Rick helped us to see the Bible as one unified story that points to Jesus.

This is what we discovered: The Bible begins in Genesis with the story of a creation that has fallen away from its Creator. Humanity has lost touch with the very relationship that defines its condition. The Creator is not satisfied with this status quo and sets about restoring his creation. From the book of Genesis to the book of Malachi, the entire Old Testament is composed of many stories, songs, and instructions which largely can be confusing and difficult to read. But when you understand the context of the writings, you begin to see these broken pieces of glass form a stunning mosaic. A picture begins to develop of a Savior for a humanity in desperate need of salvation. For the barren, he will be like a son; for the faithful, he will be like a priest; for the lost, he will be like a shepherd; for the nations, he will be like a king. All of these images come together to create one grand image that seems to match only one man.

When we got to the New Testament and read the story of Jesus, it was like all the switches flipped. Everything clicked and made sense. One of the best descriptions of the Bible's narrative technique that we have ever heard comes from our friend and mentor Timothy Keller. Keller is a *New York Times* bestselling author and the founding pastor of Redeemer Presbyterian Church in Manhattan, where he led for twenty-eight years. During a sermon, he related this example from the classic M. Night Shyamalan film *The Sixth Sense*. (Spoiler alert: the following quote reveals the movie's ending.)

> The illustration of a friend of mine comes from the movie *The Sixth Sense*. Okay, you can only see that movie twice, actually, because the first time you see it and then you get to the end and you find out, "Oh my goodness, there's this big shocking ending." The second time you see it you can't possibly see any part of the earlier passages of the movie without thinking about the end. Right? I don't want to spoil it for you but Bruce Willis is dead. . . . My point is once you know the ending you go to the earlier scenes of the movie and you say, "Ah, here's Bruce Willis and here's a woman, they're in the same room, and the first time I thought they were talking to each other, now I realize she doesn't really look at him." And you can't not look at every scene in light of the ending. It's impossible. John Piper says the same thing: You can't not—when you know how the story ends—look at that particular passage and say, "But wait a minute, Jesus is the ultimate example of that, whether or not the actual author at that moment was trying to get across a Messianic prophecy or not." You can't help it.[4]

There is a lot to unpack in that quote, but ultimately what Keller said has revolutionized the way that we read the Bible.

It built on what we learned from Pastor Rick. The Bible is a metanarrative. A metanarrative is an overarching narrative that is composed of numerous smaller stories, like subplots, all of which feed into the same big story. These smaller stories only ever make sense and have meaning in the context of the larger narrative. As Keller states about *The Sixth Sense*, the scene of the woman sitting in the living room with Bruce Willis only really makes sense when seen in light of the larger truth that Willis is dead. The Bible works in a similar way.

The famous story of Noah and the ark only really makes sense when seen in light of the overarching narrative of a God determined to save humanity from judgment, through the faithfulness of one man. When the flood comes and destroys the earth, the ark is the salvation of Noah and his family. The rainbow is a promise from God to humankind that never again will the world be destroyed by water. Through continuous cycles of rebellion, then judgment, then salvation, God rescues humanity again and again after they rebel against him. One of the major plot points in this narrative, which really sets the tale of God's rescue into motion, is the moment when God stepped into the story of his people, Israel, as an unlikely hero and saved them in the unlikeliest of ways.

The story of Moses and the exodus is the subject of the film *The Ten Commandments* and Ridley Scott's film *Exodus*. It is the story of a man who is adopted into royalty and then run out of the kingdom. This man becomes a shepherd and goes on to deliver his people from the bondage of slavery. He is a mediator between these people and their God. These people, the nation of Israel, are warned by God to sacrifice a spotless lamb and wipe the blood of the lamb over their door to be spared God's judgment. After God judges the Egyptians, Moses leads Israel through the waters of the Red Sea, and they embark on a journey to the promised land.

That story may sound interesting and even inspirational, and we have been enthralled watching Charlton Heston and Christian Bale act out the part of Moses. But what made that story come alive for us was when we began to see it in light of Jesus. Like Moses, he was in a kingdom (heaven), was sent down to earth, and served as a mediator and a deliverer for all of humanity by sacrificing his own life that all who believe in him might be spared God's wrath. The exodus was foreshadowing God's plan to save humanity through one man, Jesus Christ.

The story of Jesus, his death on the cross, and his resurrection from the dead is believed and affirmed by a majority of Americans. According to Barna, "Surprisingly, the most significant Bible story of all—'the story of Jesus Christ rising from the dead, after being crucified and buried'—is also the most widely embraced. Three out of four adults say they interpreted that narrative literally (75 percent), while only one out of five said they did not (19 percent). This is remarkable. Although millions who believe in the fact of the Resurrection may not understand how to connect the dots to their daily lives, the Bible's record of these events powerfully resonates with them even today. The window of believability is still open for millions of people."[5]

You may be in the 19 percent who do not believe the story of Jesus to be literal, or you may be in the 75 percent who do believe it. The key to understanding the Bible's message is to connect Jesus' story to the broader narrative of the Bible, which pivots on this story. All of the stories in the Bible point to this one man, and each Old Testament story fits neatly into the story of the life and work of Jesus. Once you see this, it is almost impossible to unsee it. It transforms the Bible from a collection of inspirational stories to a record of one inspirational man. Each story finds its end in Christ, and once you see him, you begin to see every story in Scripture in light of the ending.

THE UNFAIR TALE

When I (Michael) was in the eighth grade, one of my favorite classes was art. Not necessarily because I was a young da Vinci. I was more like a young Picasso, but no one seemed to appreciate my, um, unique perspective. Art class became a relaxing hour to decompress and express myself, in part because my art teacher had a unique way to keep middle schoolers quiet and focused. While we painted, drew, or sculpted, he would read to us. In eighth grade we read *Moby Dick*. Herman Melville's epic tale of Ahab, Ishmael, and the great white whale made a lasting impression on me. There was a certain sense of fairness that resonated in the story, about a man obsessed who ultimately was overcome by his obsession.

One of the greatest objections to the Bible is that it is unfair to humanity. All of us have an instinct for fairness and right and wrong; this instinct is often apparent from early in our lives. We are quick to object if we think we are being unfairly punished or wrongly accused. Much like *Moby Dick*, the Bible tells the story of humans obsessed with sin and evil and how they are continually being overcome by their obsession, portraying us all as guilty before God and in desperate need of rescue. Many object to this characterization, and people feel it is unfair that from the outset we are all declared guilty and in need of salvation (Rom. 3:23). But if we accept the rules of the story and see the narrative from the viewpoint of Christ, the story begins to change.

The story of the Bible is unfair, tremendously unfair. The story is about one who is guiltless who is declared guilty, one who is blameless who is assigned the blame of others, one who is innocent who dies in the place of those who are at fault. If any one of us were called on to assume such guilt and blame, we would object and fight to our dying breath to vindicate our good name. Yet the unfairness seen in the story of the Bible is not an unfairness toward us but an unfairness toward God.

A blameless God creates humanity, which unfairly rejects its Creator. In story after story, the Bible's narrative is the same: God rescues his people and they reject his rule. And every rescue, from the flood to the exodus to the lions' den, is foreshadowing the greater rescue to come. Arguably, God's people do not deserve to be rescued, and if any one of us were in God's place and were rejected by those we love, it would be very difficult for us to turn the other cheek and bear the cost to restore the relationship. Yet this is what Jesus does. He leaves heaven and comes to earth. The Creator walks among his creation. The gospel writer John records that Jesus came to his own and was rejected (John 1:11). His own creation did not recognize him (v. 10), but still he came. He "did not come to be served, but to serve, and to give his life as a ransom for many" (Mark 10:45).

This is perhaps the greatest misunderstanding about the Bible today. Properly read, the Bible should not make anyone feel mighty about their own life. The Bible is a raw, honest account of our failure as a people and as individuals to live well. When well-meaning people today, in the name of the Book, tout their own behavior to claim the moral high ground, they are actually undermining their argument. We naturally read ourselves into any story as the hero. But the Bible, with unexpected ruthless consistency, reminds us we are the problem.

The story of the gospel, the story of Jesus, is incredibly unfair. God takes this unfairness on himself, suffering the punishment that we deserve. You may not feel we deserve to be punished, you may not feel it was necessary for Jesus to die, but surely you find that story at least a bit compelling. This is what J. R. R. Tolkien described as a eucatastrophe. A catastrophe is a sudden calamity or downturn in a story; a eucatastrophe is a sudden reversal of fortune, a happy ending. If we were writing the story, we would want to see those who are guilty be punished, and those who are innocent be freed. But the Bible turns this on its head, saying that God's love is so great that he, who is innocent, is willing to be punished so that we, who are guilty, may be freed (2 Cor. 5:21). This is the ultimate happy ending, and it is a message which is meant not only to inspire us but also to shape and give meaning to our lives. There is a word for this, when we get what we do not deserve, when we are treated fairly when we have not earned fairness. The word is grace.

You may have had some interaction with the Bible. You may be familiar with it, may have grown up with it, may have rejected it in skepticism or ignored it in indifference. Whatever your relationship to it is, we want to invite you to take another look. The Bible is a classic, because it is never finished saying what it has to say. Perhaps before rejecting its meaning, you could try to understand its message. We believe our generation is remarkably gifted to identify timeless beauty when they see it. When you catch a glimpse of the Bible's message firsthand, you may wonder how you didn't see it before. When you come to it on its level and accept the rules of the text, when you are open to seeing Jesus as the source of the Bible's inspiration, the center of its narrative, and when you recognize how God displays his grace toward us, then and only then will the Bible begin to open up to you. The Bible does not point us to a rulebook or inspiration we might have expected. It provides the grace we most desperately need.

Baptist; yet whoever is least in the kingdom of heaven is greater than he. 12 From
of John the Baptist until now, the kingdom of heaven has been subjected to violenc
violent people have been raiding it. 13 For all the Prophets and the Law prophesied
. 14 And if you are willing to accept it, he is the Elijah who was to come. 15 Whoever
, let them hear. 16 "To what can I compare this generation? They are like children si
e marketplaces and calling out to others: 17 "'We played the pipe for you, / and you
dance; / we sang a dirge, / and you did not mourn.' 18 For John came neither eating
king, and they say, 'He has a demon.' 19 The Son of Man came eating and drinking,
say, 'Here is a glutton and a drunkard, a friend of tax collectors and sinners.' But wis
oved right by her deeds." 20 Then Jesus began to denounce the towns in which most
acles had been performed, because they did not repent. 21 "Woe to you, Chorazin! W
Bethsaida! For if the miracles that were performed in you had been performed in Tyre
n, they would have repented long ago in sackcloth and ashes. 22 But I tell you, it wi
e bearable for Tyre and Sidon on the day of judgment than for you. 23 And you, Capern
you be lifted to the heavens? No, you will go down to Hades.[e] For if the miracles
e performed in you had been performed in Sodom, it would have remained to this da
I tell you that it will be more bearable for Sodom on the day of judgment than for
At that time Jesus said, "I praise you, Father, Lord of heaven and earth, because you
den these things from the wise and learned, and revealed them to little children. 26
her, for this is what you were pleased to do. 27 "All things have been committed to n
Father. No one knows the Son except the Father, and no one knows the Father excep
and those to whom the Son chooses to reveal him. 28 "Come to me, all you who are w
burdened, and I will give you rest. 29 Take my yoke upon you and learn from me, for
tle and humble in heart, and you will find rest for your souls. 30 For my yoke is easy
burden is light." 12:1 At that time Jesus went through the grainfields on the Sab
disciples were hungry and began to pick some heads of grain and eat them. 2 Whe
risees saw this, they said to him, "Look! Your disciples are doing what is unlawful o
bath." 3 He answered, "Haven't you read what David did when he and his compan
e hungry? 4 He entered the house of God, and he and his companions ate the consecr
ad—which was not lawful for them to do, but only for the priests. 5 Or haven't you
he Law that the priests on Sabbath duty in the temple desecrate the Sabbath and ye
ocent? 6 I tell you that something greater than the temple is here. 7 If you had kn
t these words mean, 'I desire mercy, not sacrifice,'[a] you would not have condemne
ocent. 8 For the Son of Man is Lord of the Sabbath." 9 Going on from that place, he
their synagogue, 10 and a man with a shriveled hand was there. Looking for a re
ring charges against Jesus, they asked him, "Is it lawful to heal on the Sabbath?"
l to them, "If any of you has a sheep and it falls into a pit on the Sabbath, will you not
l of it and lift it out? 12 How much more valuable is a person than a sheep! Therefor

PART 2

WHERE WE ARE FROM

The Bible and History

CHAPTER 5

MILLENNIALS AND HISTORY

History will be kind to me,
for I intend to write it.

—WINSTON CHURCHILL

Both of us are blessed to have grown up in multigenerational families. Both of us know and have known our grandparents and our parents well. We spend holidays together and all live within a few miles of each other. We realize this makes us sound like we are from the 1950s, but we want to assure you we buy our clothes; we do not knit them. American families today are marked by distance, geographically and often emotionally. This was not always the case, and it is still not representative of many cultures around the world, in which generations of families live together and the young are mentored by the old. More and more millennials in America are experiencing that reality, as some 34 percent continue to live with their parents into adulthood.[1] Although some have criticized this recent shift, others have supported this cultural trend, expressing the value in maintaining close ties to family and connections to other generations.[2]

Every generation comes preloaded with a bias to think they are the first. The first to experience life as they know it, the first to truly undergo hardship, the first to really experience excitement, the first to grapple with truth. While this thought is common, it is far from correct. One of the beauties of spending time with mentors from older generations is that you realize how much you share in common. How their life experiences, whether twenty years or fifty years ago, mirror your own. The more you understand from older generations, the more you can be in touch with the history around you, and the less likely you are to see yourself and your generation as the center of that history.

Part of maturing, or "adulting," is finding your place in the grand scheme of things, finding your role in history. This is a journey we all must embark on, and it is a journey that takes us through our culture, our heritage, and the symbols of our society.

As I (Lauren) think about this process of maturing, I think of stained concrete floors. Cold, hard, gray concrete floors, polished to shine every day, despite the hundreds of feet that trample their surface daily. They are the floors of the warehouse where I work. I grew up in Oklahoma City, and in a family that owns and operates a family business—Hobby Lobby. The corporate headquarters has more than ten million square feet of offices and warehouse facilities, and in all of the warehouse space you will find stained concrete floors. The building felt like another home. Because my dad worked at the corporate office full-time, I assumed he loved being in that building, so I decided I loved being there too. It felt safe, familiar, and exciting. I remember on weekends going with my dad to the office and roaming around the massive, empty warehouse. My siblings and I would bring Rollerblades or hop on a pallet jack and use it like a scooter. To me, that warehouse, with its long stretches of smooth floor, was a playground.

As I grew up, my interactions would change. In high school, I interned every summer at the corporate office, with youthful energy. I walked across that pavement, excited to feel that I was a part of something bigger. Once I finished my undergraduate degree, I took my first full-time job at the corporate campus, and I walked across that familiar concrete like it was leading me toward vast career opportunities that lay ahead. It was not only a place I felt held opportunity for me if I just worked hard; it was also a place where those ahead of me had invested their lives. My grandfather and father had both spent their entire careers there.

As I entered my late twenties, I began to walk across that concrete with a different kind of attitude. Now that I've experienced disappointments and failures in my career, the steps I take across the worn but pristine concrete feel different. I feel the weight of responsibility. I have a better understanding of the complexity of a family business. I have years of my career behind me, and know what it means to question them. I walk those halls more prayerfully now than I used to. It is a part of the journey toward maturing. You may have felt this in your life, especially in a familiar place. It is easier to see the change in yourself when you are surrounded by an environment that has stayed exactly the same. Those corporate warehouse halls, with that cold, gray concrete, were where I once played, where I was once full of wonder, where I once held youthful optimism; now they seem different. Now they represent hard reality. They haven't changed. I have.

Though Michael and I each have had our own experiences that have shaped and matured us, we recognize that we still have a long way to go. If you're expecting us to tell you we have found our place and you should follow us there, you're reading the wrong book. We are traveling this journey today. Some mornings, we wake up with a sense of urgency about our work and a sense of meaning in our lives. Other times, many other times, we pull ourselves out of bed and commute to jobs we're not sure we are properly equipped for or truly passionate about. Yet in the midst of this drab daily routine, we have found inspiration in the mundane, ordinary lives of the majority of people in the Bible. While there are some tales of extraordinary events glistening within the pages, the Bible is mostly about normal people like us and their search for meaning in life.

So we'll be the first to admit: like we said in chapter 1, we have a bias when it comes to the Bible. We've been raised in Christian homes by families who have been passing on their love of the old-time religion to us since we were born. We do not pretend to be a high and mighty voice with credentials that offer the final, authoritative, decisive word on the subject. We do care deeply about people, and we have found the Bible to be an incredible source of hope, as well as complexity, joy, sorrow, inspiration, and frustration. But the reality is, you are who you are in large part because of who you have chosen to listen to. We simply offer a perspective from within our generation that we find to be underrepresented in the culture.

Our bias is a culmination of our beliefs shaped by our experiences, both positive and negative. We all have bias, because we each have unique experiences. No one has the same story as anyone else. So it makes sense that each of us would have a unique view of the world. Yet it is important for us to be a well-rounded generation. And for that, we all need to hear perspectives with which we disagree.

Lauren's grandfather has a saying he's never afraid to share when he feels like we need a little perspective in our lives. This dignified-looking man, head rimmed with white hair and face framed with dark glasses, with a gentle Oklahoma twang and a glint in his eye, tells us, "Only two things in this life are eternal—the Word of God and human souls." We get that to some of you that might sound simplistic, but there is a wisdom and a truth to both elements in Grandpa's words. Every soul has worth and value, whether the culture recognizes this or not. According to Christian tradition and teachings, every soul is also eternal. While this may sound like a no-brainer, we'd also like to suggest that every generation must also contend with the Word of God, the Bible. Given its outsize cultural and historical impact, it is a Book that is ever present and ever relevant. Its message and perspective are too powerful, too life changing not to engage with it, regardless of what personal conclusions emerge from such engagement.

For years, we have had the opportunity to travel the country, speaking about the Bible and the Museum of the Bible, which opened in Washington, D.C., in the fall of 2017. Throughout our journeys, we have had numerous discussions with friends, family, and followers on social media about faith and the Bible. After weeks on the road and more conversations than we can count, we noticed a theme emerging. While many young adults are familiar with the Bible, insofar as they know it exists, few read it regularly. Even fewer can answer basic questions about this remarkable Book.

When we entered into dialogue with college students and young professionals about the surprising drop in Bible engagement, they usually expressed one of two kinds of objections to the Bible. The first was based on what they had picked up from the popular culture, in which the Bible, and Christians who read and live by it, are depicted as outdated and even menacing. These negative portrayals often discourage young adults from reading the Bible, let alone believing that it is a legitimate source for wisdom and guidance.

The second kind of objection was rooted not in poor cultural perception but in negative personal experience. They had grown up with the Bible or had been part of the Christian culture but at some point had been hurt, offended, or even rejected by that culture, so they no longer trusted the Bible, which is both unfortunate and understandable.

Maybe you resonate with one or both of these types of objections. Since we have heard enough of them from our fellow millennials, we feel it necessary to explore why they are so important to our generation and to offer an alternative perspective. While part 1 of this book was devoted to defining our generation, parts 2 and 3 will address these two kinds of objections, in the hope that we can challenge our own bias and spur honest discussion among those curious about the Bible.

CHANGING PERCEPTIONS

The Bible was written thousands of years ago, but for most of history it was not nearly as accessible as it is today. During the Middle Ages, Bibles—indeed all books—were rare. To possess one was the privilege of the few and the powerful. Churches would chain a copy of the Bible to the pulpit, where it would remain under guard between readings. Such efforts became less and less necessary with the invention of the printing press in the mid-1400s. The Bible could finally be mass-produced and distributed. It was a turning point in the Bible's history.

In 1816, Elias Boudinot founded the American Bible Society (ABS) with a grand, audacious vision: to produce copies of the Bible and distribute them throughout the ever-growing cities and frontier of America. Boudinot was no revolutionary, nor was he a cultural outlier; he was responding to a need of his time. People were desperate for copies of the Bible, and in a pre-Amazon, pre-internet, indeed pre-bookstore era of American history, they had few options. So ABS produced and distributed millions of copies of the Bible. They passed them out on Manhattan street corners and sent them by the case across the new American frontier. The Bibles were not only distributed but also read.

Within the first century of its existence, the American Bible Society distributed more than two million copies of the Bible domestically and nearly eighteen million copies globally.[3] But they accomplished far more than just disseminating the Good Book: their efforts led to nothing short of a religious revival in America throughout the nineteenth century. Truly remarkable considering the limits of technology at the time. It is no exaggeration to say that during this time, the Bible was a must-read for many in America.

Fast-forward another hundred years. In 2016, we were living in New York City, where we often rode the subway to and from meetings. Often, while walking down the steps into the subway at Grand Central or Columbus Circle, we would see individuals trying to hand out Bibles. I never once saw anyone interested in the literature. Everyone was so disinterested, those Bibles may as well have been invisible.

The symbolism of this scene gripped us. Here was a Book once loved and lauded, now forgotten, and in the very city that was responsible for sending it throughout the entire country. Thousands of people every day were walking by with barely a hint of interest in this text. My grandfather's saying stuck with us, though, and we understood the longevity of the Word of God. One would think that after all of the technological advances and all of the cultural changes since 1816, perhaps the Bible would have merely vanished. Yet here it was! Whether it is on a bookshelf, on a smartphone, or even being handed out at a subway station, the Bible will often find you before you find it. The Bible has influenced our world so thoroughly in various areas of society that it can feel hidden in plain sight. Sometimes, though, it will jump out and catch our attention when we least expect it. It's hard to ignore it forever. And when the Bible's influence does show up, we have to wonder, *What are we missing by not being more engaged with this Book?*

While the common millennial narrative is that we neither engage with nor appreciate the Bible, previous generations had similar struggles. We can use several metrics to determine a generation's Bible engagement score. Sociologists can measure the frequency of religious service attendance, prayer, and Bible reading. From the greatest generation (those born 1900–1929) to the silent generation (1929–1945) to the baby boomers (1946–1964), each generation shows a higher level of Bible engagement.[4]

Perspective is important, and looking at our generation's history and the history of past generations and how they interacted with the Bible is what gives us perspective. Many would criticize millennials for their apparent abandonment of religion and their lack of interest in the Bible. Many more express concern about a rise in their skepticism toward the Bible and Christianity. Search Amazon and you will see several books devoted to diagnosing the spiritual condition of this generation, proposing solutions, and speculating about the future of everything from politics to pastimes if something does not change.

Michael and I have seen firsthand how past generations viewed the Bible. We were both raised in households that made the Bible a part of daily life. Our parents read the Bible to us when we were children, and they purchased Bibles for us when we were still in elementary school. When I was a little girl, I would wake up and head downstairs early in the morning to prepare for school, and the light in my father's study would always be on. There he would be, reading the Bible before heading to work. At night, he would read from the Bible to me and my siblings before we went to bed. Not only that, he would go so far as to record himself reading the Bible to us if he knew he was going to be out of town. Michael's parents would read to him and his brother from *The Storybook Bible*, a condensed and abridged copy of the Bible.

Our parents had learned this appreciation for the Bible from their parents, who modeled for them this level of engagement. Now, we recognize that our families are unique when it comes to Bible engagement and that your family may look very different. We know because we've heard a broad spectrum of views on the Bible from our friends and fellow millennials. Each of them had their own unique interactions with the Bible, or very little interaction at all. Our experiences in hearing their stories back up the research.

Whether we were traveling across the country or abroad, living in New York or Oklahoma, interacting with young people at a music festival or PhD students at a summer Oxford program, we loved getting to know the perspectives that shape people's views of the Bible. This generation is certainly not monolithic. During these interactions, though, we've noticed how the Bible is seen as something that is less threatening. Meaning: since it is less of an authority in culture, it is therefore less of a threat in determining our generation's trajectory. On the whole, the situation is clear: millennials appear to be firmly planted in a broader culture that no longer holds the Bible in high esteem.

IS OUR GENERATION UNIQUE?

When I (Michael) was a student in high school, I was such a perfectionist and so committed to the assignments and getting them right that I would often complete an assignment but fail to turn it in because I feared that it might be incomplete or imperfect in some way. It wasn't enough that class rules required that I turn the assignment in; I wanted to make the choice, and I wanted to be sure. I realize now that in my own way, I was living out values that are common in our generation.

Millennials exhibit a similar level of thoughtfulness and caution. Tom Brokaw, the author of a series of books on the greatest generation (our grandparents' generation), calls millennials the "wary generation." He rightly observes, "Their great mantra has been: challenge convention. Find new and better ways of doing things."[5]

We see this tendency to challenge convention in many areas of our generation. For millennials, it is not enough to simply state that this is the way things have always been done. We want to know why, and we want to know the purpose behind the choices we make.

One of the ways millennials are challenging convention, it appears, is in their approach to religion, Christianity, and the Bible.

- Forty-one percent say that they pray daily.
- Forty percent state that religion is important in their lives.
- Thirty-seven percent describe themselves as having a strong religious affiliation.
- Twenty-seven percent believe the Bible to be the literal Word of God.[6]

These statistics paint a clear portrait of a generation disinterested in religion in general and in the Bible in particular. Every older generation scores far higher in each of the areas measured. On the surface, this would seem to indicate that we are outliers, that the younger generation is sharply divided from previous generations in terms of religion. But do these stats spell out a future for us as an irreligious generation with no use for the Bible?

THE SAME KIND OF DIFFERENT AS ME

Michael's family loves to watch home movies. At times during the Christmas holiday, we've gathered around the TV, in front of a fire, and laughed as we watched a young Michael stumble across the screen or play with his new toys he opened for his birthday. One thing we have noticed as we age is that when we watch these films, we will catch glimpses of Michael's parents in the background. While they are dressed slightly differently, we realize that in some of the videos, Michael's parents were the same age then as we are now. It's a humbling thought, and perhaps you have had it: the realization that your parents and even your grandparents, who have always occupied this space in your life as older and more authoritative adults, were just as young as you once. It's one of those lightbulb, circle-of-life moments when you realize that despite our apparent differences, we are really more similar than not.

The same held true in our research. When we pored over the statistics recording how various generations interact with religion, the results filled us with wonder and no small measure of hope for our supposedly secular generation. We discovered that while millennials are more secular and less religious than boomers or gen Xers, those generations, when they were our age, had many of the same attitudes that millennials do now. Looking at a Pew Research study conducted in 2010 on religion among millennials, we identified two metrics in which this trend was apparent. Pew examined the importance of religion among the generations, as well as the frequency of daily prayer.[7]

The research showed that only 40 percent of millennials viewed religion as important to their lives, as compared with 52 percent of gen Xers and 60 percent of boomers. But if you look back twenty to forty years to when gen Xers and boomers were the same age as millennials are now, you will see that their levels were almost as low if not lower. When baby boomers were in their teens and early twenties, only 39 percent viewed religion as important to their lives.

The similarities are just as stark when you look at frequency of prayer. Pew asked the various generations how often they prayed, and scored their responses. The same spread appears: 40 percent of millennials prayed daily, as compared with 52 percent of gen Xers and 60 percent of boomers. While some would decry the difference between the prayer habits of millennials and those of boomers, when you look back to when boomers were the same age that millennials are now, the percentage of boomers who prayed daily was also in the 40s. So what does all this mean? We have drawn two conclusions that are relevant to the current conversation about the Bible and religion in culture.

The first conclusion is that while each generation may be different, in some ways millennials are the same kind of different as those generations that have come before us. The skepticism that so many in our generation, and perhaps many of you, have in regard to the Bible and Christianity is by no means unique to this stage of life. This should inspire some humility all along the age spectrum. For older generations who are quick to judge millennials and write them off as secular and even amoral, these statistics serve as a reminder that they too were once as many of us are now—questioning and curious. For millennials who are navigating the issues of faith, these statistics remind us that we did not invent the religious wheel. We are not the first generation to look at religion and the Bible with skepticism and even doubt. We are not the first generation to be confronted with the truth claims of the Bible, and we will not be the last.

The second conclusion is that the future of biblical faith is promising. Someone once said that demographics are destiny, and as we look at the trends of every previous age group, we see that as generations age, they invariably become more open to faith and more consistent in their displays of faith. As Christians who want to see more and more people read the Bible and come to know the hope it offers, we are encouraged by the prospect of more and more of our generation warming to faith as they age. That is not to say that we expect our generation to inevitably embrace the Bible in the coming decades, but it is to say that we were interested to find that previous generations had a similar starting point in their skepticism about the Bible.

As you have matured, you have probably evolved in your thinking on a range of topics, whether it be global warming, racial justice, immigration, abortion, same-sex marriage, your favorite sports team, or your taste in music. We all need the courage to change our mind when confronted with new data. Just because we are part of a generation that tends to view the Bible and faith with skepticism, does that mean we must be locked into this opinion forever? Given that every generation before us had the same skepticism and questions about the Bible yet shifted to embrace it, maybe there is something to this Book and this faith thing that we should pay attention to. What have you to lose by exploring it, even now?

We recognize that many of you who are reading this are not a part of our generation. We share your passion for Bible engagement and your concern for emerging adults. Allow us to make an appeal. We need you. We need you to invest in us through a genuine relationship in which you are not a teacher grading us on our beliefs. No, we need a loving mentor who can walk with us through legitimate questions we have concerning the Bible. Millennials will disengage if honest questions are considered a lack of faith. The Bible can handle our questions. We hope this book will encourage our generation, with the help of yours, to take a step toward engaging with God's Word.

CHAPTER 6

THE BIBLE'S IMPACT

The teachings of the Bible are so interwoven and entwined with our whole civic and social life that it would be literally—I do not mean figuratively, I mean literally—impossible for us to figure to ourselves what that life would be if these teachings were removed.

—THEODORE ROOSEVELT

The King James Bible of 1611 includes passages of outstanding literary merit in its own right . . . but the main reason the English Bible needs to be part of our education is that it is a major source book for literary culture.

—RICHARD DAWKINS

One bright April day in 1995, shortly after classes began at 9:00 a.m., we felt the ground shake in our elementary school classrooms. The vibration was not one of the earthquakes that we are accustomed to here in Oklahoma. It was the concussion wave from a massive truck bomb that had exploded outside the Murrah Federal Building in downtown Oklahoma City. What followed was memorialized on television and in other news coverage as our city began to pick up the pieces and our country began to grapple with the largest domestic terrorist attack in our nation's history. The Oklahoma City bombing was the most devastating attack on America since Pearl Harbor.

The OKC bombing would have been the generation-defining act of terror were it not for what happened another morning six years later, on September 11, 2001. When the second plane struck the World Trade Center and it was clear that this was no accident, our eighth-grade hearts lurched at the thought of a terrorist attack happening again. At the time, we did not have the language to process what was happening in our psyche. Everyone at school was in shock. Televisions that typically sat unused in the corner of the classroom were all turned on to news channels chronicling the day's horrific events.

I (Lauren) remember hearing, over our school's loudspeaker, an announcement that something bad had happened, and the school had a moment of prayer.

After the announcement, my teacher told our class what had happened. It was beyond comprehension. I couldn't even imagine it. It wasn't until later, when I watched the news coverage, that I would have the image of those two towers crumpling to the ground seared into my memory forever.

Throughout the day, I remember, every class was somber. Many parents picked up their children from school early. All that anyone could think to do was be near their families and be grateful we still had the chance to hold each other in our arms.

Both events—the Murrah bombing and 9/11—played a crucial part in the formation of both of our understanding of our society. Not so much the events themselves, tragic as they were to witness and live through, but for the responses to both events. The reaction of a culture to trial and tragedy often tells you more about that culture than the tragedy itself.

In both cases, in the aftermath of horror, we witnessed the coalescing of our society around the ties that bind. Flags were flown, churches were filled, and attendance at memorial services was higher than at most sporting events. Prayers were uttered, hymns were sung, and as our nation mourned, our leaders quoted Scripture with the ease and freedom of a preacher. Now, you can be cynical and say that these reactionary "revivals" were short-lived; you could argue that those politicians were pandering to a nation in mourning. But you would be hard-pressed to argue that there isn't an instinctive religious reflex in this country, especially when tragedy strikes.

We are not arguing that the existence of this reflex is a reason to believe in the validity of religion or that simply because some people turn to faith in times of crisis, you should as well. Instead we want to draw your attention to the reason why so many turn to faith for comfort. We want to examine why anyone would turn to Christianity for solace and support, and why the Bible is so often a source of words for those speechless with grief.

To answer these questions, we should consider the Bible's impact on our culture. You may not agree with the Bible, you may not believe in or read the Bible, but it would be intellectually dishonest to say that the Bible has not had a transformational effect on our culture. Some can, and have, pointed to the Bible's explicit imprint: biblical quotations on buildings, "In God We Trust" on the currency, "one nation under God" in the Pledge of Allegiance. However, there are threads of biblical influence woven deeply into the fabric of our society. Some are fairly obvious, some are more subtle, but there is no doubt that the tapestry of America, and indeed Western culture, would not be the same without them.

We have been privileged during the past several years to do advocacy work for the Museum of the Bible in Washington, D.C. We were the hype team, raising awareness with friends and partners who we thought might want to know about this new project. It afforded us the chance to travel and speak to small groups, large groups, and any size group that would listen. Along the way, we spoke about the vision of the museum, why the museum is important, and what people could expect when they visited.

In the museum, which opened in 2017, an entire floor is devoted to the Bible's impact, and there is even an interactive virtual reality ride that explores the Bible's influence on our nation's capital. We encourage you to explore the museum! But for now, we want to narrow the focus to three issues the Bible has had an impact on: human rights, social justice, and religious freedom. These issues are not random. They represent the heart of what concerns our generation. The value of the individual, justice for the oppressed, and the freedom to believe whatever we choose are mainstays of our generation—and, coincidentally, hallmarks of biblical ethics.

HUMAN RIGHTS

In his book *The Rise of the Nones*, former seminary president James Emery White explains the growing phenomenon of individuals who claim no religious preference. As we mentioned, nones profess no religious faith or identity and therefore have little use for religious texts like the Bible. They often claim to be atheistic, agnostic, or just spiritual. White's book is an insightful resource for grasping the shape and impact of this growing demographic within our country.

One of the trends White outlines is the growing importance of the "cause." The cause is the effort or movement that serves as the rallying point for this generation's nones in their desire to change society. This can be a global initiative to eradicate hunger or poverty, or a campaign to end sex trafficking. In the 1990s and early 2000s, generation X responded to the idea of community, which is why a careful observer would have seen a rise of "community groups" in churches. Being personally connected and part of a group was the important thing; it didn't matter whether that group was engaged in activism. Not millennials. They desire less to be part of a physical group or community than to be part of a cause. Our community is global and online, accessible 24/7/365. We have reaped the fruit of this new digital community and now have friends across the globe whom we partner with, share insights with, and mobilize with for activism.

In this day of hyperconnectivity, community in one form or another is almost a given; what we see now are those communities roaming in search of a cause. The number of efforts, hashtags, and trending topics that become the cause of the week is immense. But if we were to categorize all the movements and initiatives, most would fall under the label "human rights."

When we use the phrase human rights, we echo the United Nations' definition: "Human rights are rights inherent to all human beings, regardless of race, sex, nationality, ethnicity, language, religion, or any other status. Human rights include the right to life and liberty, freedom from slavery and torture, freedom of opinion and expression, the right to work and education, and many more. Everyone is entitled to these rights, without discrimination."[1]

The UN's definition is comprehensive and helpful and, we hope, matches your own conception of human rights. The linchpin in this definition is the word *inherent*. Meaning: these rights are part of what it means to be human; they exist regardless of whether they are recognized by a government, and they exist for every person without discrimination. Governments or groups that fail to recognize these rights are violating one's intrinsic rights. The idea of human rights places the worth of those being governed above the power of those governing.

As simple and clear as that might seem, the freedom to exercise these human rights is by no means a given in our world today. For anyone who has grown up in America, like we have, the concept of human rights is second nature. But we have to admit that even within the borders of our country, the ability to enjoy these inherent rights varies greatly depending on where you live, who you are, and what your ethnicity is. As white kids from the heartland, we realize that our experience of human rights is vastly different than it would be if we were African Americans living in Detroit or Hispanics living in Phoenix. All Americans have the right to move about free of harassment, but we have never been pulled over by a police officer for no reason or had someone use racial slurs and tell us to go home because we were members of a minority group. It pains us to know these experiences are common and all too real.

Our hearts break, as do the hearts of many in our generation, when we see the rights of those around us being trampled and ignored. Whether you support Black Lives Matter, the fight to end sex trafficking, or the pro-life movement, the root of each of these causes is the inherent right of us all to live and to live free. What unites these issues under the banner of human rights is the principle of equality and, more specifically, equal worth. So you may be asking yourself, *What does this have to do with the Bible?* We have wondered this ourselves. Has the Bible had an impact on human rights? Would our views about human rights be different if the Bible had never existed?

Many look across the political and historical landscape of the United States and criticize Christians for supporting slavery or segregation, and they incorrectly conclude that because some Christians owned slaves or supported segregation, it must therefore be part of the Christian faith or found in the Bible. Nothing could be farther from the truth!

We are not here to defend what some Christians have done in the name of Christianity, nor is it possible for us to address every wrong that you may have experienced at the hands of "Christians." We readily admit that indefensible acts have occurred in the name of the Christian religion, not to mention the Bible itself. Men and women have often misused the text of Scripture for their own gain. This is inexcusably wrong. Instead we want to look at the Bible for what it says, and it never condones the violation of human dignity. Our desire is to draw your attention to the fact that the concept of inherent human rights is inherently biblical. This concept is not new. America's founding was rooted in the belief that human rights are inalienable and are endowed to us by our Creator.

The Bible begins with the story of creation. God speaks the

universe into existence. Within that story is the account of the creation of humankind. According to the Bible, above and beyond everything else God made, humans are special, his crowning achievement! The book of Genesis records the moment when God decided to create human beings: "Then God said, 'Let us make mankind in our image, in our likeness, so that they may rule over the fish in the sea and the birds in the sky, over the livestock and all the wild animals, and over all the creatures that move along the ground.' So God created mankind in his own image, in the image of God he created them; male and female he created them" (Gen. 1:26–27).

According to the Bible, humans are different because, unlike all the other creatures on the planet, we are created in God's image. Everyone bears what Christian teaching calls the *imago Dei*—Latin for "image of God"—and therefore are often referred to as image bearers. For this reason, humans have worth; they have value over and above anything else in creation. When this notion is applied to ethics and human rights, it is revolutionary.

We are all made in the image of God. This is what makes our worth and our dignity inherent and inseparable from who we are, whether governments recognize human rights or not. We do not have rights because we deserve them; we do not have rights because we have earned them; we do not have rights because we are white or black, male or female, American or Chinese. We have rights because each of us is made in the image of God and therefore has inherent worth and dignity.

Yet this truth hasn't always been self-evident or widely believed. Throughout history, various cultures have recognized the rights of the few—perhaps only men, perhaps only white men, perhaps only landowners. In ancient Greece, the birthplace of democracy, men were viewed as having rights, while women and children and non-Greeks were viewed primarily as property. It is in Christianity and, more specifically, in the Bible that we find the source of universal human rights. All humans are created in the image of God—this is the abolitionists' argument for the dissolution of slavery. All women are created in the image of God—this is the argument of women's rights advocates for equal pay and voting rights. Children are created in the image of God—this is the argument against child labor. For pro-life advocates, this truth extends even into the womb, as they argue that every fetus is a human being, an image bearer in utero, and therefore is deserving of freedom and life.

Although it may be easy to take these rights for granted or to think that they are merely part of what it means to be Western or American, the roots of basic human rights are found in the assertion that every person has inherent worth because every person is made in the image of God. The late Dr. Max Stackhouse, professor and director of the Kuyper Center for Public Theology at Princeton, put it this way: "Intellectual honesty demands recognition of the fact that what passes as 'secular,' 'Western' principles of basic human rights developed nowhere else than out of key strands of the biblically rooted religions."[2] This biblical foundation for human rights also serves as the basis for modern ethics and the concept of social justice.

JUSTICE FOR ALL

Few causes animate our generation like issues of social justice. Once we acknowledge that every individual has inherent human rights, those rights must be protected by law. But as we have seen over the course of human history, there are times when the law denies protection to those most in need of it. Many horrendous actions have at one time or another been sanctioned by the law. So how do we decide which laws to keep and which to overturn? Simply because some prejudice remains legal, that in no way makes it right.

One of the reasons the Bible is valuable is because it reveals the moral character of God, and in so doing, it reveals the kind of moral character he intended for the people he created. If humans are made in the image of God, then it is reasonable to think that part of bearing his image is to act in a way that reflects his character. We will see that the God of the Bible is just, condemns evil, and has compassion for victims.

The Bible reveals a God whose character remains consistent and whose desire for justice remains clear. This revelation exists above both personal and legal opinion on social issues and serves as the ultimate source of appeal when at times we just get it wrong.

Martin Luther King Jr. recognized this. He was jailed in Birmingham, Alabama, for exercising his constitutional right to free speech and for fighting for the freedom of an oppressed class of citizens. King could not appeal to the crowd for justice; in his case and during his time, he could barely appeal to the courts. King did what many in the past have done when earthly justice was denied them: he appealed to a law which transcends time and supersedes secular authority. He wrote, "How does one determine when a law is just or unjust? A just law is a man-made code that squares with the moral law, or the law of God. An unjust law is a code that is out of harmony with the moral law . . . an unjust law is a human law that is not rooted in eternal and natural law. Any law that uplifts human personality is just. Any law that degrades human personality is unjust. All segregation statutes are unjust because segregation distorts the soul and damages the personality."[3]

It is hard to underestimate the impact of the Bible on this particular episode in American history. King, a Christian preacher, confronted the human rights violations of his day with an appeal based not on common consensus but on a higher truth rooted in the character of God as revealed in the Bible.

The influence that the Bible has had on our culture is difficult to ignore. However, you may not agree with this characterization of history, and you may not share our opinion of the Bible's importance in regard to social justice or human rights. In fact, you have the freedom to disagree with us. And it is to that freedom, religious freedom, we now turn.

FREE TO (DIS)BELIEVE

One of the common criticisms we have heard in our travels and in the many discussions we have had across the country is that the Bible is a source of oppression and that Christians are always trying to force their faith on others. Christians are often portrayed in media as being pushy, demanding contrarians to culture, protesting the rights of others and seeking everything from limits on sex to censorship. Many have told us that they feel Christians who engage in the public square and attempt to influence public policy do so in order to compel everyone to believe the way they do.

We are sensitive to this criticism. As we consider the way Christians have engaged with society and culture, we cannot deny that the motives of some in the public square might align with those accusations. But what we want to do here is ask you to begin to separate what some people claim is biblical from what the Bible actually says.

Among other things, this country was founded on the desire to exercise freedom of religious expression. Waves of people left Europe and other shores where religious belief and practice were controlled by the church or the state, and they came to the New World to read and apply the Bible according to their personal convictions. And as our nation began to formalize our freedom, it became law that the state shall "make no law regarding the establishment of religion and the free exercise thereof."[4]

Since the founding of this nation, Christians have advocated for an opportunity to be heard, free from governmental, religious, and societal constraints. We wish for an opportunity to offer up the truth we have found in the Bible, and it is up to you to take it or leave it. Christianity is strengthened, and the Bible is in no way limited, when other religions have the same access to the marketplace of ideas that it has. If we could whisper one thing into the ear of every culture warrior, it would be that it is not necessary to limit others in order to be heard.

Dietrich Bonhoeffer, a German pastor and theologian who was executed by the Nazis for his part in an assassination plot against Adolf Hitler, wrote extensively about Christian freedom, Christian engagement on the world stage, and the importance of a free exchange of ideas. He wrote, "The essential freedom of the church is not a gift of the world to the church but the freedom of the Word of God to make itself heard." What he is saying here is that the Bible has its own authority and its own freedom. The truth found in the Bible needs only to stand and be presented. Faith is not faith when it is forced on you; that's coercion.

We believe that when you read the Bible, you will encounter a narrative being offered to humanity rather than imposed on it. This narrative is the essence of every religious freedom we see protected in our form of government and practiced in our culture. To those who critique Christianity as stifling, and to those who use Christianity to stifle the voices of others within the marketplace of ideas, we say, "Go to the Bible." Jesus does not travel from town to town demanding that everyone believe in him. Rather, time and again, we see him arrive on the scene, proclaim his message, heal the sick, and extend an invitation to follow him. Jesus says in the Bible, and by extension to you and me, "Come to me, all you who are weary and burdened, and I will give you rest" (Matt. 11:28).

Whether you choose to believe the Bible or not, whether you choose to read it or not, there is little cause for doubt that the Bible continues to have an impact on our culture. There are reasons, beyond mere habit, why it is a source of comfort in days of national strife and mourning. There is a reason why you can find it behind the scenes, supporting the structure of our society. We would like to propose the radical idea that the Bible is a unique text that is more than just another book, more than a mere collection of stories; it is a revelation of divine character.

CHAPTER 7

WHAT MAKES THE BIBLE UNIQUE?

Without dignity, identity is erased.
—LAURA HILLENBRAND, *UNBROKEN*

A thorough knowledge of the Bible is
worth more than a college education.
—THEODORE ROOSEVELT

We were raised in the heart of "Christian America," what's often called the Bible Belt, where churches frequently outnumber bars, and almost everyone from police officers to schoolteachers seems to attend church. Many of my (Michael's) public school teachers went to our church or some other church in the area. Public prayers were offered prior to football games, and even civic events were marked by a nod to Christianity, be it a prayer, pledge, or some explicit mention of God. This wasn't just back then. Before tip-off at every Oklahoma City Thunder basketball game, heads are still bowed as a faith leader from the community leads the eighteen thousand gathered in prayer.

When we were growing up in this environment, there was a palpable respect for and a special attention given to the Bible. Seemingly every home we visited had at least one Bible, if not multiple copies. Most homes also carried the crown jewel of Bible collections: the family Bible. This was a specific kind of Bible that had been passed down through multiple generations, with a record of the family in the first several pages, recording births, marriages, and deaths.

Carrying a Bible with you to church was normal. I was unaware of the unspoken expectation until I visited a different church with a friend of mine. I walked into a classroom, and I was the only person who had brought a Bible. It was just a *habit*. The Bible was everywhere, and everywhere we went, we took the Bible.

We saw the Bible shape and transform the lives of elementary and high school students all around us. In 2002, when we were in junior high, our lives were rocked by the death of a young man in our community named Justin. Justin was a star baseball player at Yukon High School, an outstanding athlete with a .492 batting average who was named the Oklahoman's Player of the Year in 2002 and was bound for elite college ball. On June 3, while Justin was on his way home from work, the wheels on a forty-ton semi came loose and barreled toward his Jeep Cherokee. Justin swerved to the right, fatally taking the brunt of the collision and saving the lives of his fellow passengers.

Everyone loved Justin; he was kind, generous, winsome, and selfless to the end. Following his death, our youth pastor, Chris Wall, discovered Justin's journal. Now most teenagers, if they keep a journal, would freak out at the idea of anyone reading their innermost thoughts. And typical teenage journals (and we can speak from some experience, as we may have had a few ourselves) are filled with the sweet nothings of childhood, youthful complaints and angst, crushes and heartbreaks. What Chris discovered in Justin's journal, though, was unique. The pages were filled with Scripture. Page after page of his own prayers, and passages from the Bible, meditations on their meaning and impact, and personal challenges from their application. In the final six months of Justin's life, he had spent time with the Bible every day. The journal he left behind served as a window into his faith.

The afternoon of Justin's funeral, the church pews were packed. Loved ones shared what Justin meant to them. When Chris walked up to the stage to speak, he carried Justin's journal with him. Chris read several passages from the journal, including one haunting entry Justin recorded weeks before his death: "There will come a day when we will all see God face to face. This is when we will understand things fully. When God asks me to believe something that's beyond belief, I decide if I will trust my five senses or have enough sense to believe in Him."

After reading from the journal, Chris drew a line from this young man's time studying the Bible to the way he lived his life. This conclusion was not lost on me (Lauren) as I sat through that funeral. It challenged me to learn that a teenager, just like us, had actually read the Bible and was applying it to his life. It's one thing if your parents tell you to read something; it's completely different if your friends are reading it too.

Chris Wall took Justin's journal and turned it into a book, *A Life Worth Following*, which allows readers to journal alongside Justin and explore their own spirituality and relationship with God. The proceeds of the book are given to a memorial charity which provides baseball clinics for underprivileged children.

Why are we telling you all this? Justin's death and memorial service became a catalyst for our interest in the Bible. In the years since his death, we have endeavored to learn about, and understand the significance of, this Book which seemed to have marked Justin's life. We have devoted a number of years and multiple degrees to the study of the Bible and its impact on culture. One of the conclusions we have drawn from this study and observation is that the Bible is utterly unique among the texts which influence our lives.

In the previous chapter, we drew attention to the Bible's contributions to human rights, social justice, and religious freedom. The impact the Bible has made on our world is matchless. The Bible stands alone; no book can rival its cultural imprint. But here we want to look at three specific ways in which the Bible is unique, worthy of the attention of a teenage kid like Justin Sullivan, and worthy of yours too.

UNIQUE AS A BOOK

Over the course of our lifetime, as the digital revolution transformed the way we read, what we watch, and how we learn, the function of books has changed considerably. The heyday of books began around 1450, when Johannes Gutenberg invented the printing press. That invention allowed books to be spread to the masses, radically changing the relationship people had with ideas and information. For the next five hundred years, books persisted as the dominant means of dispersing information and communicating ideas. The twentieth century brought radio, TV, and finally, in our lifetime, computers and the internet. Before most millennials reached puberty, computers had begun to replace books as the primary means of learning. By the time millennials entered the job market, the digital revolution had placed a smartphone or a tablet in nearly every hand, granting 24/7 access to a world of information.

We have read a number of articles describing the end of the book as we know it. While we think this is a bit of an exaggeration, even the casual bystander would notice the demise of chain bookstores and the rise of Amazon and digital content. Throughout all this change, one thing has remained the same. The Bible remains the top-selling book year after year, maintaining its status as the best-selling book of all time. One hundred million copies of the Bible are sold or given away every year, with sales in the US totaling between $425 million and

$650 million annually. The Bible has been translated into 2,426 languages and dialects, which covers 95 percent of the globe.[1] This is a unique profile for a book in the twenty-first century, one that provokes strong opinions about it either way.

In a recent study, the Barna Group, in partnership with the American Bible Society, found some fascinating insights into views of the Bible in America.

- Most Americans (including a majority of young adults) believe the Bible has been more influential on humanity than any other text.
- A majority (also including young adults) believes the Bible contains everything a person needs to know in order to live a meaningful life.
- Two-thirds of all Americans hold an orthodox view of the Bible, that it is the actual or inspired word of God.
- Nearly half read the Scriptures at least once a month.[2]

Few if any books have or will come close to sharing this demographic profile. Whether you agree with, believe in, or have ever read the Bible, it is hard to ignore the cultural evidence that this Book holds a unique prominence among other books in our world today.

The Bible has been fought over, bled for, banned, and widely translated. Regardless of the race, ethnicity, or socioeconomic status of the reader, the Bible seems to find a relevance and a prominence that are not only cross-cultural but transcultural, surpassing the limitations of culture. It does not belong to the West, where it has prospered, nor to the East, where it originated; it is a universal story, because the God who inspired it belongs to no one culture.

UNIQUE AS A RELIGIOUS TEXT

One of the most interesting classes we took at the University of Oklahoma was a class in comparative religion. As we mentioned in the beginning of this chapter, our childhoods were steeped in Christian culture. Some may even call what we experienced a sheltered upbringing, and we would not argue. That changed in college, an intellectual challenge that we anticipated and even relished. We chose to attend a public university and take classes taught by professors we disagreed with, because we did not want to spend our lives in a bubble. We craved confrontation. Not for the sake of reckless argument and personal confusion. This appetite for intellectual sparring was birthed from a conviction that if what we believed was true, it could stand the test of the best thinkers.

We shuffled into Burton Hall to sit at desks near the middle of the room just before Professor Boyd's class was set to begin. We pulled out our laptops and prepared to take notes. Professor Boyd began. "Did you know the original drafters of the Constitution and the Bill of Rights would crap and cuss and have sex just like you and me?" Dr. Boyd would draw attention to how foundational these documents are to our society, yet point out that the men who wrote these documents were not superhuman.

Our class began to nod along as Dr. Boyd drew his conclusion. "These documents go almost universally unquestioned in our country today, and yet these men had no more right or authority to establish our society than we do today. There could be a better unwritten document to establish our government inside of you." Dr. Boyd's well-timed, well-planned lecture unexpectedly swerved from politics to religion. "Yet why do we not apply the same logic to the Bible?"

Class continued, and we were exposed to arguments, new to us, about how the Bible was composed and canonized. Dr. Boyd would go on to claim that the Bible's unreliability and its many flaws were recognized by every true scholar. For the first time in our lives, this Book that we had trusted and that we viewed as distinct from other religious texts was put side by side with the Qur'an, the sutras, and the Bhagavad Gita.

We were challenged and we were convicted. We needed to learn more. We wondered, *Is the Bible as he says, just another religious text, no different than the others? Does it have authority and power over us only because of an unspoken cultural commitment to it, à la the Constitution? Why has no one ever told us of the differences that exist between ancient copies of the Bible?*

The first thing we learned that distinguishes the Bible from other religious texts had to do with authorship. The Bible itself claims that "all Scripture is God-breathed" (2 Tim. 3:16),[3] which is to say that the Bible is inspired by a single source—God. Yet we believe that God also worked through a number of human authors over the course of fifteen hundred years to produce the various books and letters which compose the Bible. Despite that apparent diversity, we find that the Bible contains a remarkably consistent narrative, a single grand story of God's interaction with his creation.

The Bible, which was written by multiple authors, stands in contrast to the Qur'an, whose sole author was the prophet Mohammed. It also stands in contrast to the chief Hindu texts: the Bhagavad Gita, written by the guru Vyasa, and the Vedas, written by Brahma. Even the main Buddhist text, the Pāli Canon, was written by a single council in the first century BCE. Yet the Bible was produced over many centuries by a number of authors, few of whom knew each other. We are astounded at the single story found in the Book. This unity tells us that the Bible is what it says it is: uniquely God's Word to us.

The second major distinguishing feature of the Bible is that, unlike many other documents, it is a narrative rather than a list or a prescription. Contrary to what you may have heard, the Bible is not a set of rules to which you must conform. It contains no prescribed path of enlightenment or set of hoops you must jump through in order to be a believer. Through story, it models for you the way of Christianity. It introduces you to the idea that God is not an impersonal being nor a force of energy. Rather he is an eternal being whom you can know personally. He is a father to the fatherless, a brother to the lonely, and a savior to those in peril. Christianity is far more about familiarizing yourself with God than about familiarizing yourself with the practices of Christianity.

UNIQUE AS A RECORD OF HISTORY

Some years ago, we were in Cambridge, England. We were visiting friends and spending some time at Tyndale House, a study center at Cambridge University for understanding the Bible. Nestled in this historic city, with its cobblestone streets, limestone edifices, and picturesque river, Tyndale House is a leading biblical research organization. It is impossible to spend time there without being confronted with the historical impact of the Bible. Cambridge University itself was chartered in 1231 by royal decree of King Henry III, and at the time, it consisted of a number of monasteries, churches, hospitals, and convents, all dedicated to the Christian faith.

At the University of Cambridge, there are a number of

ancient libraries, including the Wren Library at Trinity College. This library has rows and rows of books; its catalog includes ancient manuscripts, copies of Milton and Isaac Newton, and even medieval copies of the Bible. It struck us that even among a collection like this, many like our professor in college would cast the Bible as just another historical text. They teach the Bible as they would teach any other book from antiquity, as a relic and as an example of a different time, with little relevance to our world today. While we agree that the Bible is a historical document and that it records the history of the Jewish people before and after the time of Christ, we would argue that the Bible is unique as a record of history.

Because the Bible records the story of an eternal God, who is without beginning and without end, there is a timelessness to the Bible's narrative and to its impact. The Bible speaks to themes that cycle through world history—life, death, and resurrection. Here we find the pattern for how life is meant to be. We can always find parallels between the story of God and the story of us. Cambridge, organized twelve hundred years after Jesus walked the earth, is a perfect example of the Bible's unique contribution to human history. Reliance on the Bible for knowledge of God so impacted medieval Britain that it produced Oxford University and then Cambridge. Four hundred years after Cambridge was founded, a young minister graduated from Emmanuel College in Cambridge, traveled to Boston, Massachusetts, and founded Harvard College. John Harvard was a Christian minister who, after emigrating in 1637 to America, where he pastored a small church, deeded his land and library to what became the college and university that bears his name.

The Bible records the history of a man, Jesus; a movement, Christianity; a nation, Israel; and the world itself. It is timeless, because it stands as part of history while also standing apart from history, recording what was before the calendar was born and prophecies about what will remain long after the calendar disappears. Because the Bible points beyond our time, it continues to have relevance to our time. It speaks of a future which still awaits humanity, and an eternity which awaits every living soul on earth. Unlike many of the books which line library shelves, whose truths and perspectives have long since passed into irrelevance, the Bible has endured and maintained its prominence, even in an increasingly secular America.

The vast majority of Americans recognize that even among other religious texts, there is something unique and sacred about the Bible. Two-thirds of Americans believe that the Bible is in some way inspired by God, rather than merely a book written by men.[4] And two thousand years after Christ, the majority of Americans see the Bible as relevant and a necessary text for coming to a greater knowledge of God.[5] The Bible is a unique source of comfort because, compared with all other books on the market today, the Bible is the most honest about the failures of humankind. It is not a self-help book fostering unrealistic expectations and demanding change by the strength of your will. Rather the Bible is brimming with stories of men and women who fail yet are given a second chance. We love this because one of the terms we like to use to define ourselves as millennials is authentic. You will not find a more authentic ancient religious text than the Bible.

There is something unique about the Bible in terms of the history it records and the history it has shaped. Within the world of books, few even come close to having the kind of impact the Bible has had or retain their relevance for the present and their promise for the future.

Baptist; yet whoever is least in the kingdom of heaven is greater than he. 12 From
of John the Baptist until now, the kingdom of heaven has been subjected to violenc
violent people have been raiding it. 13 For all the Prophets and the Law prophesied
n. 14 And if you are willing to accept it, he is the Elijah who was to come. 15 Whoeve
s, let them hear. 16 "To what can I compare this generation? They are like children si
he marketplaces and calling out to others: 17 "'We played the pipe for you, / and you
dance; / we sang a dirge, / and you did not mourn.' 18 For John came neither eating
king, and they say, 'He has a demon.' 19 The Son of Man came eating and drinking,
y say, 'Here is a glutton and a drunkard, a friend of tax collectors and·sinners.' But wis
roved right by her deeds." 20 Then Jesus began to denounce the towns in which most o
acles had been performed, because they did not repent. 21 "Woe to you, Chorazin! W
, Bethsaida! For if the miracles that were performed in you had been performed in Tyre
on, they would have repented long ago in sackcloth and ashes. 22 But I tell you, it wi

PART 3

WHERE WE ARE GOING

The Millennial Mind on the Bible

e bearable for Tyre and Sidon on the day of judgment than for you. 23 And you, Capern
you be lifted to the heavens? No, you will go down to Hades.[e] For if the miracles
e performed in you had been performed in Sodom, it would have remained to this da
I tell you that it will be more bearable for Sodom on the day of judgment than for
At that time Jesus said, I praise you, Father, Lord of heaven and earth, because you
den these things from the wise and learned, and revealed them to little children. 26
her, for this is what you were pleased to do. 27 All things have been committed to n
Father. No one knows the Son except the Father, and no one knows the Father excep
and those to whom the Son chooses to reveal him. 28 "Come to me, all you who are w
burdened, and I will give you rest. 29 Take my yoke upon you and learn from me, for
tle and humble in heart, and you will find rest for your souls. 30 For my yoke is easy
burden is light." 12:1 At that time Jesus went through the grainfields on the Sab
disciples were hungry and began to pick some heads of grain and eat them. 2 Wher
risees saw this, they said to him, "Look! Your disciples are doing what is unlawful o
bath." 3 He answered, "Haven't you read what David did when he and his compar
e hungry? 4 He entered the house of God, and he and his companions ate the consec
ad—which was not lawful for them to do, but only for the priests. 5 Or haven't you
he Law that the priests on Sabbath duty in the temple desecrate the Sabbath and ye
ocent? 6 I tell you that something greater than the temple is here. 7 If you had kr
at these words mean, 'I desire mercy, not sacrifice,'[a] you would not have condemne
ocent. 8 For the Son of Man is Lord of the Sabbath." 9 Going on from that place, he
their synagogue, 10 and a man with a shriveled hand was there. Looking for a re
ring charges against Jesus, they asked him, "Is it lawful to heal on the Sabbath?"1
to them, "If any of you has a sheep and it falls into a pit on the Sabbath, will you not
of it and lift it out? 12 How much more valuable is a person than a sheep! Therefore

CHAPTER 8

SHOULD I READ AT ALL?

———

A classic is a book that people praise, but do not read.

—MARK TWAIN

You ever talk about a movie with someone who read
the book? They're always so condescending. "Ah, the
book was much better than the movie." Oh, really?
You know what I enjoyed about the movie? No reading.
It only took two hours, and then I could take a nap.

—JIM GAFFIGAN

Growing up, I (Lauren) knew that my mother was a voracious reader. Even while raising me and my five siblings, she made it a point to get time with her books, often late into the night after we were fast asleep. I, on the other hand, was not at all interested. The books I read were only those that were mandatory reading for school, and even then I often didn't finish them. Then came a point in my life when all at once my reading habits changed. The strong motivating factor can be summed up in two words: a boy.

"Have you read *Fresh Wind, Fresh Fire?*" David asked me in an email one day. David was a senior at my high school. I was a freshman and had a crush on him. And because David's conversations with me often turned to books, I suddenly became more interested in reading. I hadn't heard of the title he mentioned, but it was now at the top of my reading list. Later that week, on a trip with my mom and siblings to Mardel Christian Store, I was elated to find *Fresh Wind, Fresh Fire*, by Jim Cymbala, perched on a shelf. I read the book fairly quickly. Between school, homework, and basketball practice, I found time to finish it in just a few weeks. (I needed to have something to talk to David about, after all!) It was my first nonfiction book, and I was hooked.

Though my initial motivation for reading may have been to impress someone else, my love for reading nonfiction has authentically deepened. Long after David graduated and moved on to college, forgetting all about me and our conversations about books and theology, I would remain an avid reader. It was during this season that I also committed myself to reading the Bible regularly. Reading became a source of growth, discovery, rest, and expanding my perspective, and I had many reference points from relationships in my life that encouraged my reading the Bible. But my experience may be far from what you've felt.

In the previous chapters, we have tried to address one of two common objections we hear to reading and engaging with the Bible: cultural perception. It is our hope that by sharing our story and addressing some of the culture's misconceptions about the Bible, we may have opened a window into its importance to both society and you as an individual.

In the coming chapters, we want to address the second most common objection that we have encountered during the last several years as we have spoken to groups, churches, schools, and universities. Many people have come to us and confessed that it is not just the cultural baggage associated with the Bible that holds them back from engaging with it. Many of them have personal experiences in their past—from negative incidents within families to hurtful interactions with churches or communities—that have colored their impression of Christianity generally and the Bible specifically. While we cannot right every wrong or answer every objection, we hope to draw some distinctions between the Bible and what has been done in the name of the Bible.

LIVING SET APART

Faith is personal. We'd go so far as to say that it's the most personal and intimate part of one's life. When we talk about faith and religion, we are talking about that which a person worships. When we talk about worship, we mean ascribing worth to something. You can participate in worship within a recognized religion like Christianity or Hinduism, or you can worship your relationships or your career. Everyone lives *for* something. There is a religious word that describes this well: *holy*. It means set apart, sacred, separate from everything else. So whatever you worship occupies a unique place in your life, above and beyond the rest. It captivates your heart, your soul, and your mind.

Christianity is a personal yet communal religion. What do we mean by that? Christianity is not merely an individual experience but a shared experience based on shared beliefs. No one comes to the Christian faith on their own; everyone who believes does so as a result of hearing the Word of God, most often paired with a personal invitation from someone else. Whether it is through a conversation, a sermon, a text, or a book, you receive the ideas of faith from some outside source.

The apostle Paul, writing a letter to the church in Rome in the first century, described the process this way: "How, then, can they call on the one they have not believed in? And how can they believe in the one of whom they have not heard? And how can they hear without someone preaching to them?" (Rom. 10:14).

One of the limitations of the Bible is that it must be read or heard. In order for the life-changing message to transform an individual, that person must engage with it personally. Yet there is a chasm of two thousand years between us and the last contributions to the Bible. How are we to approach a book that was completed not just before the founding of America but more than a thousand years before Columbus?

READING RITUAL

Michael and I are passionate about brunch. We have a deep-seated dedication to our Saturday morning brunch ritual, which we zealously protect. We tend to work late nights throughout the week, so on Saturday morning, we sleep in as late as we can and wake up hoping we have missed the early morning brunch crowd. It is never a question of if we will go to brunch, only where. One of the benefits of coming of age at the dawn of the iPhone revolution is the gift of digital search engines to identify great brunch spots. One of the benefits of marriage is getting to split one sweet and one savory brunch plate. Often, Michael will order eggs Benedict and I will order French toast, my favorite. The best of both worlds!

One Saturday morning after brunch, we got into our car and drove to Cuppies and Joe, our favorite coffee shop in Oklahoma City. Actually, as we write this story, we are seated at our favorite spot in Cuppies and Joe: the front room by a window. Most Saturdays, regardless of where we are in the country, when we have free time, you can typically find us sitting in some local coffee dive, reading. We love to read together. Sometimes we are reading the same book for a course we are both taking; sometimes we are immersed in different books, reading for pleasure. Sometimes (rarely) we are reading fiction. One of the truths we have learned during the past ten years of college and grad school is that reading may not always come easy, but if it is cultivated as a skill, it can mold and shape you in ways you never thought possible. And while we often sit in silence across from one another, we have found that the act of reading together has brought us closer to each other as a couple.

One Saturday morning, we were relaxing in the sunlit

front room of Cuppies and Joe. Steam was rising off our cups of freshly poured coffee, and a partially eaten treat sat on the table between us. We were both reading a book called *The Intellectual Life* by A. G. Sertillanges. While this book has been almost continuously in print since 1934, it's not particularly well known. The book is often assigned by graduate schools and seminaries to incoming PhD students, as was the case with us. There are many truths in this book that have left an impression on us, but a few stood out in particular. As we sat in the coffee shop, we shared a moment when what we were reading struck us.

Sertillanges, a French priest, was concerned with cultivating the mind through learning and discipline, and he believed that the universal means of learning was reading. While he devoted almost an entire chapter to the art of reading, this particular paragraph impressed us both. "Choose in your books—not everything is of equal value. Do not on that account assume the attitude of a judge; be to your author rather a brother in the truth, a friend, and even a humble friend since, at least in a certain respect, you are taking him for your guide. The book is your elder; you must pay it honor, approach it without pride, read it without prejudice, bear with its faults, seek the grain in the chaff. But you are a free man, you remain responsible; hold back sufficiently to keep possession of your own soul and if need be to defend it."[1]

There is much in this quote that strikes at the heart of our current culture and our generation. Words printed on the page used to be taken as nearly certain truth. Today they seem only to carry doubt. The source, and any implicit bias it carries, has to be weighed. The millennial generation has learned to doubt. But not all reading is problematic. Not everything is of equal value, but it takes effort to sort out the bad.

Despite the challenges, we see that contrary to popular conceptions and critiques, millennials are readers. According to the latest Pew Research Center data, millennials read more than any other demographic. In fact, according to Pew, "Younger adults are more likely than older adults to read for work or school, or to research a topic of interest."[2] They are also more likely to read for pleasure; 83 percent of eighteen- to twenty-nine-year-olds read for pleasure, more than any other demographic. While we find this encouraging and, as a couple, find ourselves comfortably inside this trend, the quote we read that day struck a chord with us for the following reason.

Sertillanges is advocating more than merely letting the words pass in front of your face; he is promoting discernment and humility when reading. Reading is of value only if you value the process enough to do it thoughtfully. We have discovered four easy principles, based on Sertillanges' statement, that we follow to help us evaluate what we read and determine what is important and what is not, which has crucial implications for the all-too-obvious question, Is the Bible itself worth reading?

1. *Recognize that not everything is of equal value.* This is especially true today in the information age, when we have more knowledge at our fingertips than any previous generation ever had. Simply because something is in print does not mean that it is worth our time and effort to read and take to heart. Not every link is worthy of a click, and not every book is worthy of a full and thorough read. We have all fallen victim to clickbait. We have all read down an internet wormhole of articles that looked interesting, but said nothing. Consider the source, and consider your goals. Is what you are about

to read from a reputable source? Is it a classic? Or is it classically flawed? The English philosopher Francis Bacon offers some helpful insight here: "Some books are to be tasted, others to be swallowed, and some to be chewed and digested: that is, some books are to be read only in parts, others to be read wholly, and with diligence and attention."

2. *Approach the book with humility.* The old adage "Never judge a book by its cover" is simple but helpful. Sertillanges suggests that we approach books as humble friends rather than judges. There have been many times when people have recommended books to us and we have not found them particularly helpful. Other times, society and culture might decry a book and criticize it, but we have found it useful. One of the most common traits shared by young adults is that we are allergic to being judged or prejudged. No one deserves to be cast aside based on first impressions. Books are similar. A frequent critique we have of many within the Christian community is their tendency to react to what they dislike and to censure what they disagree with, often without ever reading, watching, or investigating for themselves. Allow yourself to be surprised from time to time, and do not be shut off from the possibility of learning something new, based solely on the opinion of others.

3. *Recognize the value of others' hard work.* It takes an immense amount of work to produce a book. Authors do not work alone; they are accompanied by editors, publishers, and often researchers. It can take more than a year to produce a book of any consequence, and some books are the result of decades of work by authors who

have poured their hearts and souls into their work. There is a reason why some books are viewed as dangerous, and some as monumental; they may contain ideas that can change a reader's mind and by extension change the culture and the world. Let's face it, we are shaped and mentored by what we read. Whether it is Shakespeare or Stephen King, Jim Collins or Oprah, you are who you read. So read wisely and recognize that when you read, you are being mentored by someone's hard work and scholarship.

4. *Read discerningly.* One of the greatest tests of truth is its ability to last. The classics of literature are classics because they speak to the human condition and communicate truths that have withstood the test of time. When you choose what to read, you are well served if you can distinguish between what is principled and what is merely popular. A number of options are laid before us, a number of books we can read, but that does not mean that we should read them all or read them all equally. While some books will set you free, others can weigh you down; often, the greatest test to determine which is which is to ask, Has the truth in this book endured the test of time? We have found it most helpful to start with the classics—those great books that have added to the lives of men and women for generations and freed the minds of individuals. We also recommend considering the authors you read: Are they diverse in background, ethnicity, and gender? We have a great deal to learn from those who don't think like us. As you pick up each book, what you choose to read is helping build within you a core conception of truth; the purer the truth, the stronger

the core, and the less likely you will be swayed by every new idea that comes along.

These principles are our suggestions for how to guide your reading life. The British author Neil Gaiman has written extensively on the need to read and the value of literacy. Some years ago, he wrote in the *Guardian*, "There were noises made briefly, a few years ago, about the idea that we were living in a post-literate world, in which the ability to make sense out of written words was somehow redundant, but those days are gone: words are more important than they ever were: we navigate the world with words, and as the world slips onto the web, we need to follow, to communicate and to comprehend what we are reading. Literacy is more important than ever it was, in this world of text and email, a world of written information. We need to read and write, we need global citizens who can read comfortably, comprehend what they are reading, understand nuance, and make themselves understood."[3]

We could not agree more, which is why we are encouraged that you are reading this book, and why one of the reasons we wrote it was to spur you on to reading more in the future. Now, while these four principles are general and meant to aid you in telling the difference between the classics and clickbait, consider this: What would it look like if you applied these rules to the Bible?

WHAT IF?

What if we examined the books before us, and all the truth claims they contain, and determined that not everything is of equal value? Does a blog post hold the same weight as a book that scholars have pored over for centuries to understand? Could it be that the book at the foundation of so many organizations, the inspiration for so many stories, whose passages are etched in stone across the globe, could have something to say to each of us? It may seem difficult to read, you may not even know where to begin, but perhaps the Bible is one of those books that Bacon suggests should be digested slowly and is worth more than a passing glance.

What if we were to approach the Bible with humility, as a friend, not as a judge? You may have heard what the Bible says. You may have seen characterizations of it which cause you to view it with suspicion, even negativity. But what if instead of faking that we already know what it says, we approach it with the attitude that we may not have it figured out and that it may have something to teach us? This posture of humility can be just as difficult for those who have never read the Bible as for those who have read it all their lives. The former think the Bible has nothing to teach them because they have never even given it a chance. The latter think the Bible has nothing to teach them because they have already been through it and think they have learned all there is to know. None of us like to be prejudged; we want to be given the benefit of the doubt. And when we don't prejudge, we allow ourselves the gift of discovery. We recognize it is unfair when others assume we will be a certain way because of our age or our experience. To be intellectually consistent, we should approach books, and in this case the Bible, in the same way we would like to be approached—with an open mind, as a friend rather than a judge.

What if we viewed the Bible not as just any other book on the shelf but as the fruit of millennia of work and wisdom?

The Bible contains numerous books and letters, written by some forty authors, across three continents, over the course of two thousand years. From there, it took many years and numerous councils and printings to arrive at the text that is in the hotel room drawer next to your bed or on the shelf of your grand-parents' living room. Yet despite its long history and multiple authorship, the Bible is an astoundingly consistent narrative. We will delve further into the specifics of that narrative in the next chapter. Suffice it to say, all the effort put into making the Bible has been equaled only by the reaction to the ideas it contains. For as long as the Bible has existed, it has inspired both shock and awe. Men and women have died to protect it, and some have killed in its name. If any other book had such a history, would you not want to at least explore what is inside?

Finally, if we are pursuing truth, and truth endures, should we not at least consider the enduring truth the Bible claims to hold? Inevitably, we will be presented with truth claims and different things to believe. How do we discern which is right and which is wrong, which is real and which is fake? How do we guard against being swayed or distracted by every new post and every new idea? Perhaps there is value in rooting ourselves in a classic like the Bible. We (Michael and Lauren) have learned that when life gets messy and everything around us seems to crumble, we need something that does not change. The next iPhone comes out every single year. We long for an anchor in the storm that is unchanging, timeless, and true. And we have found that of anything we have ever read, and anything we have ever heard, the Bible is the only sure and unchanging source of truth in this life.

CHAPTER 9

THE BIBLE IS THE STORY OF US

———

[God] rewards those who diligently seek
Him, not just for one moment or one day,
but for every moment and every day.

—BARACK OBAMA

Dear Warden, you were right.
Salvation lay within.

—ANDY DUFRESNE,
THE SHAWSHANK REDEMPTION

Do you remember when you would dream of what your life might be like at a certain age? When you reached that age, were you surprised by how differently things turned out? Some would say that this experience can best be described as maturing. Maturity is the reconciliation of dreams hoped for and life lived. Pleasantly, sometimes these two things reconcile perfectly, and the life you experience is as good as or better than you ever could have hoped.

Lauren and I feel this way about marriage; we were high school sweethearts and dreamed of one day being married. The reality of our life together has been more difficult but also more wonderful than we could have imagined at seventeen. We married at twenty-one, while still in college. We took a fun vacation for our honeymoon, and it was like a dream. Once we returned home, immediately we both got sick. A few days later, we had our first "fight." A few months later and the quirks that were once cute were now annoying. Years into marriage, we hit a rough patch that left us questioning what our relationship would look like in the future. Through the journey, there have also been beautiful moments. Each time we worked through a conflict, we grew closer. We learned how to communicate with one another, we gave and received grace, and we came to believe that we truly are better together. In the space between the dream and the reality is our story, where we grow and mature.

One of the reasons we are so committed to reading generally and to rereading the Bible in particular is that immersing ourselves in a variety of stories helps inform our story. As we just examined in the previous chapter, the Bible is the singular narrative of God and his creation. But that larger narrative is composed of many micronarratives, stories we can relate to and characters we can't but empathize with. Reading about their different lives and their similar struggles, their failures and their relationship to God, the same God we know now, helps inform our life and our struggles. When we read the Psalms and see the various authors crying out to God in true honesty and vulnerability, it invites us to do the same. It gives us permission to approach God with the same kind of rawness. Or when we read about Esther as she risks her life to stand up for her people, it can provide us strength to stand up for our beliefs about what is right. There are countless ways the stories and characters in the Bible have shaped our lives and brought us comfort.

The Bible is a beautiful, unique text in that its micronarratives and metanarrative provide us with insight for life. As we sit with God's story, it not only informs us and makes us more complete; it also teaches us about the consistent character of God—his faithfulness and love, his mercy and justice. Reading the Bible gives us the opportunity to see God through the lives of others. While the times may change, and the people, the languages, and the cultures all may change, the God whom people interact with does not. There are two constants that you will encounter in reading the Bible: the first is the human tendency to fail; the second is God's steadfast love and patience. It is true that God's love is never changing. It is also true that God is just, and therefore God judges people for rebelling against him and hurting others. But that judgment doesn't discount his love; it actually makes it more real, for he loves people so much that he is willing to make things right in the world by punishing those who perpetuate injustice. The interplay between these two constants—human failure and God's steadfast, never-changing love—is what makes the Bible relevant to our lives today. Both are just as true now as they were two thousand years ago. People still fail—on that we think we can all agree. We also hope you are increasingly open to the idea that God is still faithful.

Both of these truths, these constants, are not always apparent early in our lives. Realizing both truths requires the same reconciliation between hope and reality that produces maturity. What happens when life doesn't turn out the way you thought it would, when you don't get into that school or marry that person or work that career? What do you do when people fail you, emotionally, physically, financially? Do our lives matter at all, or is it all just a bunch of nothingness, coming from nothing, leading to nothing, and in the end signifying nothing? We are all in search of solid ground. Some thing, some relationship, some job, someone to anchor our life and provide stability.

What we discover as we age is that there are very few solid rocks on which to stand. Most if not all of those relationships and jobs will shift and sink, just like sand. Many of you know what we're talking about; you can relate to a time when life stole your hope, a time when disappointment shook you to your core. We've sure had our fair share of disappointments. But through it all, the God we've discovered and encountered in the Bible has remained ever true to his Word, steadfast and never-changing in his love toward us.

A NARRATIVE TO MAKE SENSE OF OUR SUFFERING

I took Michael out to a nice steak restaurant for a meal we couldn't afford on his twenty-fifth birthday. We reminisced about the highlights of his first twenty-five years, and then we began to dream about what the next quarter century might hold.

It was then I dropped a bomb on him. I shared with Michael my desire to start our family. But my desire was more specific: I longed to adopt internationally. This had been part of my family's story, and I wanted it to be a piece of our family's story as well. The one prerequisite for international adoption we did not meet before that day was the age requirement. To adopt in many countries, you have to be at least—you guessed it—twenty-five.

I looked at him nervously, knowing the gravity of the request. But to my surprise, Michael smiled and shared with me how God had been growing his passion for our church's partnership with an orphanage in Uganda. He told me we should pray for forty days about whether to pursue adoption. I was stunned by his instant enthusiasm. I agreed to commit this dream to prayer, even though the interim seemed like an eternity. But the next day, when I got home, Michael had printed off all the paperwork to begin the adoption process. Apparently, he couldn't wait forty days either! We began the paperwork while we continued to pray that God would make clear whether this was our path. At the end of forty days, we were both confident it was.

We recently marked six years since we began the adoption process. With Uganda's shifting adoption laws, we went from a slowdown to being completely shut out, just as we were nearing the front of the line. We had peace that though this was not our plan, everything happens for a reason. With many of our friends pregnant, we decided to try to grow our family through biological children.

But eventually our excitement about trying to conceive turned into confusion about why we weren't succeeding. After a year and a half of trying, we had another significant conversation, but it lacked the optimism of our initial discussion. I took Michael to a cheap lunch and shared the medical test results: it would be difficult for us to have biological children.

Infertile. Barren. Unable to conceive children. These words sucker punched me. After the doctor called, I was reeling from a flood of questions. *Why would this happen to us? What did we do to cause this? What's the solution?*

It's puzzling to mourn the loss of something that doesn't happen. People can understand mourning the passing of a loved one. But to grieve the loss of an unrealized future is different. I became gripped by fear of the unknown. In an instant, my dreams for my family and my desire for children were in jeopardy.

In the majority of cases, our friends' desire for biological children has been fulfilled. We felt alone. Isolated. Only later would we learn that one in eight couples reports experiencing a season of infertility. The actual numbers are likely higher.

Other couples we know struggled with infertility yet now have beautiful children. We cling to these stories as a source of inspiration. But as we began sharing our experience, we realized we didn't know any couples who had shared their journey in the midst of infertility. Moreover, many people assumed we were outliers, as if infertility affects only a few. There is an unspoken shame, a fear of voicing the cold reality of barrenness. We prayerfully discussed what God would have us do. Ultimately, we chose to share our journey in the hope of reassuring others walking the same path. We wanted them to know they are not alone.

We knew we were opening ourselves up to the potential of being hurt by well-intended comments from friends, family, and others. I deeply appreciate every person who bravely offers words of consolation and encouragement. However, I notice myself and others pointing to a hope in God's power to provide rather than a trust in God's presence to satisfy. And often, God does provide; most couples' desire for children will be fulfilled by God. It's likely we will be blessed to conceive or adopt children.

As we look around our world, it is easy to see there is suffering. And much of this suffering is far worse than our childlessness. There are children without access to clean drinking water. There are nations with dictators who brutally murder their own people. There are evil men who take advantage of women for their own sexual pleasure. There are orphans who are abducted for slave labor or worse. There is systemic racism that prevents men and women of color from excelling. We could go on and on and on.

How are we to make sense of the suffering around the world? How can we reconcile the suffering we experience? While we will never fully understand the why of our suffering in this life, we all seek a larger narrative to help us comprehend it.

The ultimate hope the Bible offers to Michael and me in our barrenness and to the world in its suffering is that God is better than our circumstances. We don't need children to live a full, happy, purpose-filled life. We must have said to each other a hundred times, "We would much rather have a life without children than a life without Jesus." God's plan for us is best, even if it doesn't include the full house we envision.

This may mean that we never get to hold our own children. We may never experience a baby shower with our closest friends and family or rush to the hospital for delivery. We may miss out on sleepless nights and the sting of a teenager's embarrassment of his parents. We may grow old with no one to come visit us at

Christmastime, and die without ever giving away our daughter or giving marriage advice to our son. Our desire for children might always be unfulfilled. We continue to wrestle with this, and we do not take this unfulfilled dream lightly, though we do trust that God is the source of our hope.

A NARRATIVE TO GUIDE OUR MORALITY

Lauren and I both grew up in homes with families who loved us and raised us to love the Bible. Although getting to church was less than peaceful, still we were taken to church. Every Sunday morning, Sunday night, and Wednesday night. Our fathers both taught Sunday school. Our mothers sang in the choir. We met in Sunday school at Council Road Baptist Church in Oklahoma City. I now serve on the staff as the teaching pastor.

When I was a child, both of my dad's parents and my mom's mother went to Council Road. Not only that, my father's father's parents went to Council Road. On a typical Sunday morning in the mid-1990s, the McAfees would dominate the third pew. I grew up playing with crayons as a toddler, and singing songs out of the hymnbook as a child, sitting between my grandparents and my great-grandparents.

As a youth, restlessly squirming in the third pew, I was full of dreams about what my future would look like. Dreams of having my own family, of my parents growing old together, greeting their grandchildren, caring for one another, maintaining the stable relationship on which I had come to rely. I was always close to my parents. I enjoyed a bond with them in which I was able to share my hopes to write a book (look at me,

Mom!) and my dreams for the future (that definitely included Lauren).

Lauren and I began dating the summer before our senior year, and we enjoyed our last year of high school together, including prom. We chose to attend the same university and continued dating. But one month into my freshman year of college, I had the most jarring experience of my life.

On September 30, 2006, at 10 a.m., I received a phone call from my mother. This was odd, because my sweet mother *never* calls me for fear of being an inconvenience. When I answered, she asked me to come home immediately. This was *really* odd, because my mother had told me repeatedly when I moved to the University of Oklahoma, in Norman, that she did not want me to come home; she wanted me to establish a new life on my own.

I couldn't drive home fast enough. I don't know how I avoided a speeding ticket that Saturday morning. When I walked into our home in Oklahoma City, we began a conversation that would forever reshape my hopes and dreams for my family. My father, who had been my hero my entire life, announced to my mother, my younger brother Matthew, and me that he intended to divorce Mom, ask God for forgiveness, and start a new life.

The room began to spin around me. My father not only had vowed to Mom that he would remain faithful "for better or for worse" but also had repeatedly promised me he would never leave. There had to be some sort of misunderstanding. We began asking some clarifying questions. Mom asked him to reconsider. Matthew slumped in his chair with his head hung.

The following week, I asked Dad to meet me at IHOP. When I walked in, he was wearing his signature ear-to-ear grin and said hello to his "favorite oldest boy." But I didn't walk in empty-handed. Throughout my life, Dad had gifted me Bibles to commemorate life's milestones. There was the Bible I was given the day I was baptized. The one I was given a few years later when I asked for a wise heart for Christmas. Then I was given a Student Bible when I entered middle school. And finally, Dad gave me a Bible my senior year.

Plopping all four Bibles on the table, I pointed to the pile and asked Dad a simple question: "Where in this Book, which you taught me to live by, does it say you are making the best choice for our family?" I believe the Bible gives reasons that justify divorce, but not without serious cause. Dad's smile disintegrated. This was a conversation in a different orbit. Sometimes that happens; we all have choices to make when presented with the Bible's take on reality. My father chose to disobey the Bible's teaching about honoring one's marriage and commitment to family. Sadly, while our relationship has improved, the consequences of this choice continue to affect us all. It was and is a defining chapter of my life.

Everyone is searching for a metanarrative. A story to place ourselves within that illuminates the path forward. We want a narrative to guide our journey through life. If the world truly is nothing more than an evolving cosmic accident without consequence, then nothing I do on this planet matters. We may—we *must*—all eat, drink, and be merry, for tomorrow we die (Isa. 22:13). But something in us tells us that the way we treat others matters. When we're honest with ourselves, we know there's something bigger than us, a story larger than our own.

The Bible is that story.

The Bible is altogether different. The Bible does not explain away our suffering, nor does it deny that we are suffering. Rather it shows there is purpose in the midst of our struggle (Rom. 8:28). The Bible does not excuse our immorality, nor does it tell us to simply try harder to be moral. It points us to our inability to live perfectly moral lives, yet calls us to holiness. The Bible does not present us with a purpose for living which makes much of us, nor does it have us find our purpose in others. It points to a purpose beyond this world.

The Bible challenges us to come to the startling realization that our solo story is not the defining story after all. But then it invites us into the wondrous hope of stepping into a bigger story, a story in which we are not the lead, but in which we have always belonged. In this way, yes, the Bible is nothing we expected but everything we ever needed.

CHAPTER 10

THE BIBLE AND SPIRITUALITY

You Christians look after a document containing
enough dynamite to blow all civilization to pieces,
turn the world upside down and bring peace to
a battle-torn planet. But you treat it as though
it is nothing more than a piece of literature.

—MAHATMA GANDHI

In the day-to-day trenches of adult life, there is
actually no such thing as atheism. There is no such
thing as not worshipping. Everybody worships.
The only choice we get is what to worship.

—DAVID FOSTER WALLACE

There was a time, though neither of us can pinpoint the moment, when we became aware of something greater than ourselves. Our worlds shrank, and we felt dwarfed by the knowledge that we were not alone in existence, that our lives were caught up in a story larger than we could have imagined. It is said that when we are newborn babies, our eyes lack the ability to focus on anything a few inches beyond our face. Slowly, as our nerves mature and the muscles in our eyes strengthen, the larger world beyond the faces of our parents comes into focus.

We spend our formative years acquainting ourselves with the physical world around us, which is daunting enough, but then we become aware of something beyond the physical: the spiritual. Often, it is our parents who inform us about the concept of spirituality. In our case, our parents introduced us at a very early age to the concepts of God, Jesus, the Bible, and Christian ethics and morals.

We are grateful for their hard work at tilling the soil of our spiritual lives, but there was a moment when we took ownership of these truths and concepts for ourselves. And like many of you, who may come from different religious traditions or perhaps a nonreligious spiritual background, we view our spirituality as inviolable and sacred. If we truly own anything, it is the spiritual experience of our relationship with God, as we understand him through the witness of the Bible.

Millennials are far more open to the Bible than most people realize. Nearly three out of four millennials view the Bible as a sacred or holy book, and more than half of all millennials believe the Bible is a "comprehensive guide to a meaningful life."[1] Yet many millennials do not look to the Bible as a core part of their spirituality.

Early reports indicate a greater rise of skepticism among our younger gen Z siblings. Like many millennials, they may not view the Bible as a source for spirituality or key to a relationship with God, but that doesn't mean they don't claim to have a personal spirituality of their own. Personal spirituality is a hallmark of both generations.

After years of reading articles, interviewing peers, and engaging in conversations, we have come up with this attempt to define spirituality: spirituality is how our belief about the unseen world affects our interaction with the physical world. The exercise and development of spirituality is, in a sense, religion. The nonphysical world can be based on nature, the body, the community, or the mind—or perhaps a mix of all four. What does this look like?

For instance, Manhattan is the least Christian borough of New York City. In Manhattan, there is an antipathy toward the Bible and an aversion to the "cultural Christianity" that is dominant in regions like the South. But while this part of NYC may not be Christian, it is intensely spiritual. We saw evidence of this throughout our time living there.

We lived on the Upper West Side, and within five blocks of our apartment there were seven yoga studios, three synagogues, and three meditation centers. It seemed that everyone was living out some form of spirituality. Their physical lives were informed by a sense of purpose and meaning derived from something nonphysical.

Almost everyone we met in Manhattan had a drive for significance. They wanted their lives to have meaning and impact, even if only in some small way. We continue to see this drive everywhere we go, especially among our generation. Young adults want their relationships to matter, they want to make a difference through their vocations, and they want the tragedies in their lives to make sense. People want the events in their lives to have purpose; often, what is right in front of them, what they can observe with their own eyes (the physical), is not sufficient to satisfy this desire. When the physical fails them, they go searching for meaning elsewhere.

This is normal. Humanity's search for something outside of ourselves, and outside of the physical world, is a key indicator that there is something or someone outside the physical world we are meant to know. This drive for meaning is the greatest indicator that we are in fact created beings and that we have a Creator.

As personal and unique as an individual's spirituality may be, there comes a time in its development when the person will seek some sort of guide. At some point, when you have exhausted your own resources and experiences, you need to lean on the guidance of others. For some, the guide may be a guru, a teacher, a preacher, an imam, or a rabbi. Others may turn to a holy text: the Vedas, the Bhagavad Gita, the Torah, the Qur'an, or the Bible.

It may come as no surprise that we are going to commend the Bible to you as a resource for your journey of understanding spirituality. We believe the Bible to be a unique spiritual document, given its cultural and personal influence, in that it is a record of the spiritual or supernatural revealing itself in specific ways, with a specific identity, to the natural world. And the Bible itself, through the message of Jesus, claims to hold *the* truth—*the* answers—to our spirituality.

The Bible is a multifaceted jewel which reveals a message that is equally divine revelation, life manual, and love letter. In chapters 5 and 6, we outlined briefly how history has affirmed its spiritual influence and power. Here we want to outline how the Bible defines and shapes personal spirituality. The Bible is important not just because it defines spirituality; it is important and even revolutionary because of the type of spirituality it defines. The Bible gives us a picture of a spirituality that is mediated, supernatural, and grace-filled. Let's unpack this.

A MEDIATED SPIRITUALITY

Central Park is so named because it lies at the very center of Manhattan. While it looks pristine and natural, almost every square inch of its eight hundred acres is structurally designed and manicured. Every tree was planted with purpose, every stream plotted with intentionality, every lake and vista designed to evoke untouched nature. The designers knew that there is something special and needed about nature. People who live in planned and controlled cities need access to something that reminds them of unharnessed wildness. Lauren and I would often grab a coffee and go escape the hustle of the streets and bask in the quiet of the park with a few thousand of our fellow New Yorkers. The raw beauty of nature beckons to all humanity. Even the planners of that great city knew that everyone needs a metropolitan respite to get in touch with something we cannot control.

One of the biggest complaints we hear from our generation concerns the trappings of religion. Religion is bulky, with its buildings and rituals, priests and pastors, liturgy and candles.

Young adults want access to the spiritual apart from the baggage of religion. They want an unbroken relationship with the spiritual, and they don't want anything to get in the way.

This is one of the great appeals of practicing yoga, Buddhism, and the like. The promise of impersonal and unencumbered spiritual experience is intoxicating. It is just you and your thoughts, centered on and connected to the unseen spiritual world. There is nothing to divide you and the supernatural. This type of spirituality is more about traveling a journey than arriving at a destination. You are on a quest for meaning and connection—inside yourself, outside yourself, throughout nature and the spiritual realm—and whether you discover that meaning matters less than the fact that you went exploring in the first place. This approach boasts intriguing rhetoric but in moments of honesty leaves you with a sense of hopelessness when you hear others faking fine along their own path of loneliness.

Biblical spirituality, in contrast, is oriented toward relationship. It is far less about personal introspection and far more about a personal encounter. The God of the Bible is a relational God; to begin with, he is in relationship with himself, through the Trinity. God is one essential being but also three persons, and the relationships between them are described in familial terms. God the Father has a relationship with God the Son, who has a relationship with God the Holy Spirit, who himself relates to God the Father. These three persons exist in perfect peace and unity, hence their oneness.

This relational God also exists in relationship to humankind. This relationship in particular, the God-human relationship, forms the core of the Bible's narrative. From cover to cover, the Bible tells the story of God's heart for humanity and desire to be in relationship with them, just as he is with himself.

The Bible paints a picture of a spiritual life that is mediated. You are not left to your own devices. You are not on this journey alone. God intervenes in your journey and offers a relationship to you. You grow spiritually and experience spirituality *through* that relationship with God. The relationship is both the journey and the destination. The Bible shows us that we were created for this one extraordinary spiritual relationship. And every spiritual longing we have is a hunger pang for a relationship with God. An early Christian theologian in Africa, named Augustine, is famous for saying that our souls will be restless until we find our rest in God.

Jesus is the physical embodiment of this relationship. Jesus is God, yet he is also a person like us. Jesus comes to us and serves as a mediator between us and God; he demonstrates what a fully functional spirituality looks like. And that fully functioning spirituality is typified by his perfect and unbroken relationship with God. This relationship gives Jesus a calm in the face of the storm, and a peace and sense of purpose in every situation. Who can resist that measure of peace and certainty in life? If this kind of spirituality exists, wouldn't you want to experience it for yourself?

A SUPERNATURAL SPIRITUALITY

During the last twenty years, as millennials have come of age and barged into adulthood, with gen Z close behind, many people have attempted to indoctrinate this independent generation with new ways to satisfy their spiritual longings. Some have offered legalistic religious ideals, which countless millennials have rejected. Others have suggested outright atheism (a disbelief in God) or secularism (a rejection of religious ideas). Then there is a third way: people like Sam Harris and Richard Dawkins, atheists in their own right, have proposed an alternative answer for the spiritual drive we all possess.

When we were in college, we came face to face with this third way, this "natural spirituality," as they call it. Many of our friends were like Sam Harris: they claimed that spirituality was real and that the language of spirituality was important, but that it exists because of purely natural and scientific reasons. In his 2014 book *Waking Up*, Sam Harris describes his use of the term spirituality in this way: "I will use spiritual, mystical, contemplative and transcendent without apology. However, I will be precise in describing the experiences and methods which merit those terms. . . . Spirituality begins with a reverence for the ordinary that can lead us to insights and experiences that are anything but ordinary."[2]

For Harris and many others, spirituality comes from our observations of the world around us, and that's it. There is nothing and no one beyond the observable sphere of science and nature. One can find meaning and perhaps even purpose from these observations, but God does not enter the picture. We are in control of our experience; we are in control of everything except each other. This spirituality is tame and controllable, which deceives us with the illusion of comfort.

This differs dramatically from the picture of spirituality we see in the Bible. In this picture, we discover a spiritual world and a spiritual being, God, who exists outside of the natural world. God is supernatural, above and beyond the natural. Spirituality in the Bible begins with a reverence for the extraordinary, in this case God.

God created the natural world and as a result is in control of the natural world, the way you were in control of the Lego world you created in second grade. God can part seas (Ex. 14:21), calm storms (Ps. 107:29; Matt. 8:26), and even reverse death (Ezek. 37:5; Col. 2:12). The Bible presents to us a miraculous spirituality that goes beyond science and supersedes nature, giving us purpose and meaning when science and nature fail to provide answers. The quest for spirituality is a desire to experience a transcendent reality. What we find comforting in the Bible's picture of spirituality is that its power is outside of our control, it is bigger than us, and therefore it can deliver on its promises. The obstacles that we face in this life are immense, and often we are not strong enough to overcome them alone. Which is why we need something—someone—outside ourselves to intervene.

As I (Lauren) have experienced seasons of panic attacks, doubts about my career, and confusion about our infertility, this spirituality that brings relationship with God has been a foundation for me.

The first time I had a panic attack, I was in a leadership conference with hundreds of people sitting around me. The speaker had said something that triggered memories of a hurtful experience I'd had one year prior. All at once, I began to feel as though I were having a heart attack. I didn't know what was happening. I felt slightly dizzy, my chest was tight, and it was harder to breathe. I tried to slow my breathing and stay calm, and in the process managed to think past the fear of dying and recall the symptoms I had read in a textbook for my master's degree in counseling: I was having a panic attack.

Even though I realized what was happening, it was still scary. I sat there and didn't let anyone know something was wrong. A little while later, I left the conference, drove to the airport, and left for a business trip I had scheduled. Since that first experience, I have gotten better at telling people when I am having an attack, and I've come to rely on Scripture as a comfort when the unwelcome tightness in my chest decides to take over. Philippians 4:6–7 is one verse that comes to mind: "Do not be anxious about anything, but in everything by prayer and supplication with thanksgiving let your requests be made known to God. And the peace of God, which surpasses all understanding, will guard your hearts and your minds in Christ Jesus" (ESV).

Amid seasons of confusion, the God of the Bible offers himself as a source of meaning, of purpose, and of power that is constrained only by his character. And since God is love and is perfect in every good attribute—truth, mercy, justice, compassion—he can be trusted even when we don't understand what he is doing.

God's supernatural power means that nothing in nature can disrupt his plan or interrupt his relationship with us. The apostle Paul puts it this way: "Who shall separate us from the love of Christ? Shall trouble or hardship or persecution or famine or nakedness or danger or sword? . . . For I am convinced that neither death nor life, neither angels nor demons, neither the present nor the future, nor any powers, neither height nor depth, nor anything else in all creation, will be able to separate us from the love of God that is in Christ Jesus our Lord" (Rom. 8:35, 38–39).

A GRACE-FILLED SPIRITUALITY

Every drive that our generation has to explore spirituality and try to comprehend its importance is rooted in the need for some meaning and purpose outside of our own lives. That need is as natural and as important as breathing. The problem is that in our generation's pursuit of happiness, we do not seem to be very happy. Part of this unhappiness comes from the burden placed on us by modern concepts of spirituality: we are in charge, we are in control, we are the ones who have to find a way to peace. If we lack peace, if our lives are devoid of meaning, then we need to meditate more, work harder, commune with nature more often—the list never ends. This nonstop effort leaves us thirsty for more, never finding satisfaction.

The power of the Bible is that the spirituality it outlines is not based on our performance or ability. In America, success is a validation of one's worth that comes only through one's greatest achievements. The message of the Bible is that even our greatest achievements merely validate our imperfection; God offers us the perfection of Jesus' success in exchange for our failures. Our worth is based not on the right or wrong we do but on the work Jesus has done on the cross. Our access to a healthy spiritual life is a gift—one we do not deserve, because of our imperfections, and one we cannot afford, but it is given to us anyway. The Bible calls this grace.

Biblical spirituality is entirely grace filled. The Bible claims that God created you and fashioned you in such a way that you desire his presence and hunger for a relationship with him. When something gets in the way of that relationship, God transcends the natural-supernatural divide and comes to you. Any broken relationship requires a cost to be paid for restoration. There is either a restitution cost, where the offender pays for the wrong they committed, or there is a forgiveness cost, where the wronged party absorbs the wrong into themselves. As humans, we could never pay back God for our mistakes. On the cross,

Jesus absorbed the wrongs we have committed against God and paid the ultimate price to extend to us grace.

Our culture is based on quid pro quo. You do something for me; I do something for you. You scratch my back; I scratch yours. When we spiritualize this ethic, what results is a legalistic system that, much like karma, equips us to be kind only to those who are kind to us, and mean to those who are mean to us. This ethic is rooted in the idea that everyone should get what they deserve. The result of this kind of spirituality is that we often feel like we never measure up. Grace is different. Instead of getting the retribution we deserve (justice or karma), we get what we don't deserve: grace. Grace is what distinguishes Christianity from other religions, and biblical spirituality from secular spirituality. This picture of receiving what you do not deserve is radical and countercultural.

One of our pastors in New York City, Tim Keller, describes it this way.

> This is one reason that our religion is absolutely and utterly different from every other religion. I've been saying this for over thirty years, and I regularly look at other religions to make sure that someone won't pull a "preacher gotcha" on me: "What about this religion over here?" and I'd have to say, "I haven't heard about that one. Let me read about it." No, every other religion is like building a bridge. You build a bridge by putting pylons down, and then you build the bridge over the pylons. And if you run out of money, it's the bridge to nowhere. There are a few like that. That is what every other religion is like. It's a process in which you are trying to get over to the other side. You never feel like you have arrived, but you're trying. In every other

religion, people are trying to work their way across. Not with Christianity. One minute you're not regenerate and the next minute you are. One minute you're not adopted and the next minute you are.[3]

It is our hope that as you read these words, the truth behind them will set you free from the burden of performance that can so easily weigh you down. Your spirituality is your own, and it is precious, but it is not reliant on your intelligence, nor is it limited by your lack of talent.

The God of the Bible is one who sacrifices everything to make you his own and bring you into a relationship with him. God seeks after you in order to make you whole and complete, physically and spiritually. Jesus took our spiritual brokenness onto himself physically and allowed his body to be broken. Three days later, he rose physically from the dead to give us a new spirituality. When you receive this gift and begin to understand the way that grace works in your spiritual life, when your sense of meaning and purpose is infused with grace, everything changes.

The experience of grace in your spiritual life will never stay contained to your spiritual life. Martin Luther, the Catholic monk who upended the established church during the Reformation, did so from an understanding of grace in his private spiritual life. He wrote, "This grace of God is a very great, strong, mighty and active thing. It does not lie asleep in the soul. Grace hears, leads, drives, draws, changes, works all in man, and lets itself be distinctly felt and experienced. It is hidden, but its works are evident." Once you experience this grace, you want to share it. You feel compelled to do so because everyone, including your enemies, is just as worthy as you to receive kindness. God gave of himself for you, so how can you not give of yourself for others?

This insatiable passion to share about grace is at the core of our drive to write this book. As we sit here at our desks on a Saturday, we are not at a barbecue with friends or on a romantic getaway at some lake. We are writing late into the night with a hope of passing on the spiritual reality that has marked our lives. We do not expect to get rich and famous from this book. This work has cost us a great deal personally. But the message of grace has revolutionized our marriage, our work, our relationships, our life. We cannot *not* tell you about the grace of God in Christ.

To be honest, we have a bit of fear at this point about what you will think of us, the Bible, Christianity, and the dedicated minority of our generation who share this grace-filled spirituality we have explained. But that is the price of authenticity. And we believe that the opportunity for us to grow as a generation will be realized only when we sit down at a table and converse on a soul level. So far, when we have chosen to be transparent about our faith, we have had many more positive encounters with our fellow young adults than negative ones. We have no reason to believe this book will be any different. But the fear of rejection isn't painted over with a thin layer of experience. So if you have read to this point, thank you for listening.

We understand that this explanation of biblical spirituality may not sound like the faith you heard about when you were a child. And it almost certainly doesn't sound like the Christianity you have heard about on the news or in popular culture. Only the extreme examples of any group make headlines. We believe that what we have described is the essence of the Bible's message and the relationship God offers. You may not believe in God. We are willing to bet that if you explained to us the God you don't believe in, we wouldn't believe in that God either. The God of the Bible may not have been the God of the church you grew up in, or the God who was preached to you elsewhere. It is our hope that you will meet the God we have met in the pages of the timeless Book he has given us.

PART 4

HOW WE GET THERE

The Starting Point

CHAPTER 11

HOW TO START

Man shall not live by bread alone, but by every
word that comes from the mouth of God.

—JESUS (MATT. 4:4 ESV)

Most people are bothered by those passages in
Scripture which they cannot understand; but, as for
me, I have always noticed that the passages which
troubled me most are those which I do understand.

—MARK TWAIN

I (Michael) was given a precious gift as a seven-year-old that, to my shame, I wasted. In the mid-1990s, Santa came by my home in Oklahoma City and left a Super Nintendo. My parents connected this small gray box with two big purple switches on top to the back of the television, plugged in a couple of controllers with directional pads and little purple buttons, inserted a game cartridge, and turned on the system. The screen came up from black and read, "Super Mario Kart." Excited, I chose Mario (later discovering Yoshi was the best) and prepared for my first race. Seven computer-generated drivers were lined up, and the countdown from three led to the start of the race. That was the moment I decided I didn't enjoy video games.

Mario would not budge. I pressed forward on the directional pad, and Mario just sat there like a defiant toddler. While the computer players sped around the track three times, no matter how hard I pushed forward, Mario would not even lean forward. Months later, my older cousins came over to my house, excited to play *Mario Kart. Good luck,* I thought. *That game is impossible.* Yet at the start of the race, their characters began to zoom around the track, passing computer players on the left and right. How was this possible? What was the secret?

It turns out that in addition to pushing forward on the directional pad, you also have to push the B button with your other hand to accelerate. I know you are probably scratching the skin off your face reading this painfully obvious point I missed, but in my defense, I was the oldest child in my home when I was growing up, and I had never played a video game in my life.

If you are like us, you probably often feel like you are missing the B button in life. With social media, the comparison monster can seem to crush our progress, making us feel like we are falling farther behind others in achieving our life goals. At times, scrolling through our feed leaves us feeling like others have found some helpful life hack we missed.

You may or may not have ever felt this way about the Bible, but anyone who has tried to read it for themselves has inevitably found themselves asking, "What am I missing here?" Throughout this book, we have attempted to highlight both the soaring bliss that comes from reading the Bible and connecting it to our daily life and the sour struggle of trying to understand the Bible's difficult passages.

Chances are, if you grab the Bible and open it up without a working knowledge of how to read it, you will either open to page 1, like you would a novel, or play Bible roulette and stick your finger in the center of the Book and begin reading randomly. I had a friend who was unfamiliar with the Bible and was unemployed and looking for work. He turned to the Bible's table of contents, saw a book titled Job, and decided to read it for instruction on how to get himself hired. Little did he know that this was a story about a man named Job who loses everything he has and is left mourning, naked and covered in ashes, as he contemplates the meaning of life. My friend thought he was going to discover sound advice from the steady wisdom of someone like Danny Tanner and ended up emotionally exhausted after surviving an ancient version of *Cast Away*.

There are many books you could read that would help you read the Bible well. We want to offer a simple pattern of Bible reading in the hope of giving you a way (not the way) to engage with the Bible. In truth, there is no perfect way to read the Bible, but we hope this survey can help provide some introduction to this Book that will prevent you from losing again at Bible roulette and give you a B button aha moment to orient you to reading the story of stories.

PRAY FIRST

The first thing we would encourage you to do is pray. If the Bible is what it claims to be, written by God, then we will certainly need help from the Divine Author in understanding the Book. The Pharisees in Jesus' day had large portions of the Bible memorized, yet Jesus rebuked them, saying, "You study the Scriptures diligently because you think that in them you have eternal life. These are the very Scriptures that testify about me, yet you refuse to come to me to have life" (John 5:39–40). It is possible to know the Bible extremely well yet miss Jesus when he is speaking directly to you. If this Book is inspired by God, as the Bible-reader millennials believe, then the only way we can ever hope to understand it is with God's help.

When we pray, we typically use an acronym that is based on the Lord's Prayer.

- *P—Praise.* Take a moment to give God praise or thanks for the things he has done in your life and in the world. Also, give God praise not just for the things he has done but for the good Father the Bible says he is.
- *R—Repent.* The Bible makes it clear that we are all sinners in need of a Savior. Take a moment to confess the wrongs you

have done and the good you have left undone. Admit your need for Jesus to forgive you. First John 1:9 says he will!

- *A—Ask*. Now that you have acknowledged God as a good God and have admitted that you are in need of him, ask what you will. God cares about you and your cares. We can boldly approach God as a good Father who longs to give good gifts to his children (Matt. 7:11). Especially when we ask for things that he says, in the Bible, he wants for us.
- *Y—Yield*. After you have presented your requests, yield yourself to God. The Bible promises that when we delight ourselves in the Lord, he will give us the desires of our heart (Ps. 37:4). This doesn't mean he gives us whatever we want, but he desires for us to want what he wants to give us. Then we will be satisfied.

Following prayer, open your eyes and open your Bible to begin reading. But where do you start? How do you begin? What makes for a great Bible reading experience?

BIBLE OVERVIEW

The Bible is not one book. The Bible is many books that have been compiled into one Book of Books. Genesis, the first book of the Bible, has an author, story, and purpose that are completely different from the author, story, and purpose of Romans. These two books were written some fifteen hundred years apart. Each book is a bit different and owns a distinct role in the history of the people of Israel and the formation of the Christian church. For simplicity, we will divide the Christian Bible into five major sections.

1. *History*. Genesis through Esther documents the history of ancient Israel. It begins with creation, then moves through the patriarchs, the establishment of a kingdom in Israel, the exile to Babylon, and the return back home. Some of the stories are out of order or told more than once. Nearly the entire first half of the Old Testament (the Hebrew Bible) is documenting the story of ancient Israel.[1] Many of the most well-known Bible stories are in this section: Adam and Eve, Noah and the flood, Joseph and the coat of many colors, Moses and the parting of the Red Sea, David and Goliath, and more. This section of the Bible is largely historical narrative. We are learning how God has worked in the lives of his people, with promises made for how he will work in the future.

2. *Poetry*. Job through Song of Songs is filled with poetry. Job tells the story of one man's suffering and faith in God. The Psalms are 150 songs of praise, lament, repentance, and supplication. Proverbs is a collection of wise sayings. Ecclesiastes chronicles one man's search for meaning. Song of Songs is a story of two lovers. Poetry is meant to be illustrative and figurative in order to stimulate your imagination and get you to think in new ways about God and the way he interacts with his people. It is best enjoyed slowly, reading to savor.

3. *Prophecy*. Isaiah through Malachi is a run of seventeen prophetic books that were written at various points along the history of Israel. Prophets spoke to the people of Israel on behalf of God. While in the Bible's history section you will see many self-obsessed kings and rulers (hard for us to imagine any political leaders like that today, right?), in contrast the prophets are largely Israel's

moral and spiritual North Star. They point Israel back to God and call for repentance of the nation's sinful ways. As you might expect, there are also prophecies of things that are going to happen in the future. Some of these prophecies come to pass within a generation of the prophet, some point to the coming of Jesus, and some will not be fulfilled until the end of the world.

4. *Gospels.* Matthew, Mark, Luke, and John are the first four books in the New Testament. The New Testament is named such because Jesus has taken the old covenant, which made the Israelites the people of God, and extended the invitation to all people of all backgrounds. Each of the four gospels was written by a person who knew Jesus personally or lived closely with someone who knew him personally. They are called gospels because the word *gospel* means "good news." All four gospels say that Jesus was born of a virgin, claimed to be God, lived a life without sin, performed miracles, was betrayed and died on a cross, and three days later rose from the dead. This is good news because his resurrection gives all who repent and believe in Jesus spiritual resurrection and new life.

5. *Letters.* Acts through Revelation details what happened after Jesus rose from the dead and ascended to heaven. Acts is a historical letter sharing about the life and ministry of the early followers of Jesus, including the outbreak of persecution. In a shocking twist, the man who began Christian persecution, Saul, converts to Christianity and ends up writing more than half of these letters. Saul is renamed Paul, and all the letters from Romans to Philemon are attributed to him. The letters

of Hebrews through Revelation are written by other early leaders of Christianity to churches and individuals, instructing them how to live in light of the resurrection of Christ. Revelation is an apocalyptic vision that John receives from Jesus and is written to the church.

So where should you begin? As we mentioned, the Bible is all about Jesus. If you were reading a mystery novel, the last thing you would want to do is jump to the twist coming in the second half of the book. Yet that's our suggestion for reading the Bible.

In the Gospel according to Luke, we see at the end of the book Jesus appearing to two disciples on a road to Emmaus. Along this road, Jesus teaches them how all of the Old Testament points to him. It is only then that they begin to understand both the Old Testament and Jesus, the resurrected Messiah. It will begin to make sense to you only in light of the resurrection of Christ, the interpretive key to the Bible.

THE POINT WHERE MANY PEOPLE QUIT

Every generation has childhood sitcoms that encapsulate the adolescent experience. For millennials, one of the heirs apparent to the late gen X *Saved by the Bell* and *Fresh Prince of Bel Air* was *Boy Meets World*. This sitcom centered on Cory Matthews, whose best friend, Shawn, always had his back. In their story line, Cory was always fighting with his brother, Eric, and pursuing his romantic interest, Topanga. Every show wrapped up with a life lesson from their teacher, Mr. Feeny. In the same way that each *Boy Meets World* episode centered on Cory's witty banter with Shawn, a fight with Eric, a romantic moment with Topanga, and a life lesson from Mr. Feeny, each section of the Bible is a mixture of historical narrative, poetry, and wise teachings, building a complex and beautiful story that all points to Jesus.

If you try to understand the Cory and Topanga romance expecting Eric fights, you are going to be confused. If you give Mr. Feeny's teaching the same weight that you give the playful banter of mid-puberty Cory and Shawn, you will miss the wisdom. Point being, you have to approach each genre of literature found in the Bible with the attitude and mindfulness that the genre demands from you. Only then will you be able to place each element in its proper context.

Many people will quit engaging with the Bible when it becomes difficult. The Bible is unlike other books of our time because it speaks to us from an ancient time. Part of the beauty of the Bible is that it is timeless, yet this can hinder us from benefiting from its message. This makes the Bible both uniquely valuable to us and uniquely challenging to read. Reading in general is hard work, so we don't fault anyone who quits before they really get going because of the difficulty of reading the Bible. But we have found that anything truly valuable in this life is worth the struggle. The Bible is no different. The more you exercise, the more it pays off and the more you enjoy it. The more you practice a musical instrument or engage in conversations with strangers or paint or teach or whatever you do, the more enjoyable it becomes and the more you gain mastery of it.

R. C. Sproul called me out when I read these words of his: "Here then, is the real problem of our negligence. We fail in our duty to study God's Word not so much because it is diffi-cult to understand, not so much because it is dull and boring, but because it is work. Our problem is not a lack of intelligence or a lack of passion. Our problem is that we are lazy."[2] This is our (Michael and Lauren's) biggest obstacle to reading and studying the Bible. But we have found that when we put in the work, the payoff is more amazing than anything else this life has to offer.

Read first to try to discover what was happening back then. As you read about Abraham in Genesis, picture yourself in his world. When Jesus is telling a parable (a fictional story with real-life application), imagine yourself in the story. This is how Jesus himself understands the Bible. When questioned about divorce in Matthew 19, he asks why Moses allowed for a certificate of divorce in his day. Understanding the Bible first in its ancient setting is foundational before applying it to your life today.

After we understand what the original authors intended to communicate, we can consider how to apply this teaching to our lives today. A commonly misunderstood verse is Philippians 4:13: "I can do all things through [Christ] who strengthens me" (ESV). You may remember seeing "PHIL 4:13" written on Tim Tebow's eye black on the cover of *Sports Illustrated*. However, this verse was not written to encourage athletes that they can accomplish seemingly impossible feats if they have enough faith in Jesus. (Tim knows this, by the way.) Rather this was written by the apostle Paul, who, though he found himself writing from prison, declared himself to be content in his situation. He had learned to be content because he didn't need wealth or freedom to be filled with joy and peace or to share about Jesus with others. He could "do all things through [Christ]." Applying this teaching after understanding the original meaning encourages us to be content in whatever circumstance God has placed us in, because it is an opportunity for us to tell others about Jesus.

We have talked to some people who at this point are ready to throw in the towel. If the Bible isn't as simple as reading it and applying it directly to my life, how do I know if I am interpreting the Bible correctly? Aren't scholars unable to agree on what some of the passages of the Bible mean for us today? If these experts who study the Bible all day everyday cannot come to terms with the passages, what hope do I have?

These are honest, sincere questions. We struggle with the same thoughts regularly. However, we do not apply this same logic to other areas of our lives. There are debates about whether certain foods are good for you (we are looking at you, eggs). But we don't give up on eating. We are willing to bet that most of you eat eggs on occasion. If you do not, we also went through a vegan phase. More power to you. The existence of a variety of takes on an issue has never stopped us as a generation from forming our own. Whether it be on climate change, pizza toppings, border security, professional wrestling, gun control, or *The Bachelor*. Engage with the Book the best you can. And the best way to form a well-informed take on the Bible is to read it with people who can teach you more about this amazing Book.

So there's a lot going on in this Book! Each story is multi-layered and connected to all the others. Now let's take a look once more at the biggest game changer.

THE MOST IMPORTANT THING

If you remember only one thing about the Bible, it should be this: the Bible is about Jesus. It's not about you and me. It's not about all the individual stories that are turned into Hollywood blockbusters. They all serve the purpose of pointing us to Jesus, the same way every scene in Harry Potter serves to advance the narrative of Harry's life and struggle against Voldemort. It is only by reading the Bible through the lens of asking how it points us to Jesus that we will begin to understand the Bible as an epic with massive implications for our daily lives. Martin Luther said, "The Bible is the cradle wherein Christ is laid."[3]

THE POWER OF CONSISTENCY

You may be thinking, *I could never read the entire Bible. It's so long!* You're right! It is a long book. As a matter of a fact, the Bible is roughly eight hundred thousand words. For reference, this book is roughly fifty thousand. So imagine reading sixteen books just like this one, and you're talking about a book the size of the Bible. However, perhaps a better comparison to the length of the Bible is the Harry Potter series. If you have read all seven Harry Potter books, you have read more words than are in the entire Bible. That series is more than one million words. Well done! So can you apply the same discipline to reading the Bible? The key is to be consistent in reading small sections.

I have seen firsthand, in Lauren's life, the power of consistent time in the Bible. (She doesn't know I'm writing this. Don't tell her.) (Note: I got busted in the final round of edits, but she graciously allowed me to keep this portion in the book!) Lauren has been faithful to pray, read her Bible, and journal every day since November 14, 2003. At the time of this writing, that's more than fifteen years. Half of her life! She would tell you that this is only by the grace of God. I will add, it is by the grace of God at work in and through her. I, on the other hand, have never made it one year (maybe not even one month!) doing what

Lauren has done for a decade and a half. So don't fall victim to the comparison trap. I tell you that to share with you a powerful example of someone our age so committed to spending daily time with God in the Bible.

Lauren didn't set out with the goal of reading the Bible and journaling every day for fifteen years; she made it a goal to get into the Book today. As with any discipline, the more you do something, the better you get at it and the easier and more rewarding it becomes. When you get into the Bible, the Bible gets into you. That's why we want to end with a challenge to you. A challenge that, if you're game, could change your life.

CHAPTER 12

THE CHALLENGE

Don't let the noise of others' opinions
drown out your own inner voice.
—STEVE JOBS

He died not for men, but for each man.
If each man had been the only man made,
He would have done no less.
—C. S. LEWIS

It is not the strength of your faith but the
object of your faith that actually saves you.
—TIMOTHY J. KELLER

We have asked ourselves multiple times, as we wrote this book, if there is a single reason why you should listen to either one of us when it comes to reading the Bible. We are privileged, white, Bible-believing, evangelical, conservative Christians who were practically born wearing WWJD bracelets. Some of you are asking yourselves, *What's a WWJD bracelet?* That's exactly our point. We are full-on Christian weirdos. You might think, *Of course you believe the Bible. Of course you want me to read it; you don't know any different. You have been brainwashed since before you watched Power Rangers.* Or, like some of our friends who were raised in the faith but have long since abandoned it, you might be thinking, *I was once like you two. I used to believe this stuff. I also used to believe in Santa and the Easter Bunny and that wrestling on TV was real. But I came to my senses years ago. I gave the Bible its chance. I know what's in it, and I don't need any part of it.*

We understand where you are coming from, and we are sensitive to these critiques. We have thought long and hard about how to address your concerns. In the previous chapters, we have appealed to your sense of identity and your sense of history, hoping to articulate an argument in the Bible's favor. We have shared part of our story and told you how the Bible has defied expectations and has continually proved itself to be relevant in our lives. But as we draw to a close, we want to issue a final challenge. We hope against hope that you will take us up on this. It is not a singular challenge, as if we were simply saying, "Hey, you should read the Bible!" We want to challenge our generation and you, as readers, to live up to the hype of who you claim to be—the open-minded generation.

TRIGGERED, TEMPTED, BUT TRUE

We live in the age of the "trigger warning," something totally foreign to us millennials who graduated from college not that long ago. For those unfamiliar it, a trigger warning is a heads-up of sorts. It communicates that the content following the warning could be distressing. As we (Michael and Lauren) read the news and speak on college campuses across the country, we are noticing a curious new trend. Today colleges and universities are increasingly establishing "safe spaces" on their campuses. These spaces are necessary for human flourishing. We affirm the vital role that safe spaces and trigger warnings play for victims. Anyone who has experienced trauma or has need for proper care and space for their mental health deserves a healthy environment in which to process their pain. However, with as much passion as we carry for victims who deserve safe spaces and warnings for triggering content, we also have a healthy dose of frustration with those who are afraid of challenging conversations and true thought exchange and would shut down honest, civil debate. Freedom of speech, the freedom to exchange information, is part of what has made our country unique, and it will be what helps us continue to grow. We fully affirm the creation of safe environments to protect mental health, but we draw the line where safe spaces become death zones for any controversial topic, which can often include religion. There is a great opportunity to learn when our opinions are questioned and we are exposed to new ideas. We are concerned that some are using the term "safe space" as an excuse to avoid exposure to alternative viewpoints and not respecting these spaces for what they should be—a refuge for those who have experienced trauma.

A 2016 study by National Public Radio found that roughly 50 percent of professors issue trigger warnings prior to discussion of "difficult material,"[1] often when discussing topics of a graphic violent or sexual nature. We acknowledge that it is understandable to create safe spaces when discussing such topics, but the question quickly becomes, Does the topic of religion, or even the Bible, belong in that safe space?

A recent article in the *Atlantic* quotes Boston University professor Stephen Prothero, who observes this trend in his classroom, saying, "Students are good with 'respectful,' but they are allergic to 'argument.'"[2] The article continues:

> Religion can be an immensely important part of one's identity—for many, more important than race or sexual orientation. To assert that a classmate's most deeply held beliefs are false or evil is to attack his or her identity, arguably similar to the way in which asserting that a transgender person is mistaken about their gender is an attack on their identity. Objections to "anti-Muslim" campus speakers as promoting "hate speech" and creating a "hostile learning environment" vividly illustrate the connection between contentious assertions about religion, trigger warnings, and safe spaces. The claim that Islam—or, by implication, any religious faith—is false or dangerous is indistinguishable from hostile hate speech. To make such a claim in class is to be a potential enemy of fellow students, to marginalize them, disrespect them, and make them

feel unsafe. If respect requires refraining from attacking people's identity, then the only respectful discussion of religion is one in which everyone affirms everyone else's beliefs, describes those beliefs without passing judgment, or simply remains silent. . . . That's usually what ends up happening.[3]

Regrettably, this type of intellectual environment rarely stays inside the classroom, which makes it difficult for those who wish to have a spiritual conversation, a free exchange of religious ideas. Our culture prefers open-mindedness but often defines being open-minded as being uncritically accepting of everything. You may be tempted to think that we wish to leverage this trend in the Bible's favor and argue, "Hey, you can't critique the Bible; you have to accept our opinion, or we will get offended." We want you to know that this is not where we are coming from.

Whether you were taught the Bible by Dr. Richard Dawkins or Dr. Billy Graham, we want to challenge you to read the Bible for yourself. We do not want you to just accept our opinions. We want to invite you to challenge, test, and question your assumptions about the Bible and Christianity, to come and see for yourself. We do not want you to be allergic to argument and discussion; we want you to open yourself up to conversation about the Bible. It is a challenging Book inasmuch as it challenges your personal status quo; it makes demands on your life and promises for your future. The Bible makes universal truth claims, and therefore it will doubtless at times differ from your personal preferences and opinions. Such challenges are necessary for change, and we would argue that as our generation matures, the Bible is uniquely positioned as a catalyst for growth.

We're reminded of the scene in the beloved children's book *The Lion, the Witch and the Wardrobe* in which Susan asks Mr. Beaver a flurry of questions about the great lion Aslan. She is nervous about meeting him, so she wonders, "Is he quite safe?" To which Mr. Beaver replies, "Safe? Who said anything about safe? 'Course he isn't safe, but he is good. He's the King, I tell you."

Similarly, the God of the Bible is not safe, for he will mess with your assumptions about reality and make demands on your life. But he is good, and he is for your good. So is the Bible. It may not be made for safe spaces, but it is good space—in which to question, to wrestle, to discover.

A few years ago, Michael and I were in Vatican City for the opening of an exhibition titled *Verbum Domini*, which, translated into English, means "Word of the Lord." The exhibition, sponsored by the Museum of the Bible, profiled the Bible in various forms as it has existed down through the ages. Walking around that ancient city, we had the opportunity to see many of the sculptural works of Michelangelo, the Renaissance artist known for painting the Sistine Chapel in the Vatican. While he is famous as a painter, we discovered that he was primarily a sculptor. Vatican City is littered with his marble sculptures and statues. Our tour guides were fond of telling us the stories about his creations and about the way in which Michelangelo worked. Michelangelo believed that hidden inside every block of marble was a statue, a character that just needed to be released. The sculpting process, for him, was not about creation as much as it was about liberation. He would chisel away until the hidden figure had been freed. Sculpting is a violent confrontation between stone and chisel, but this conflict is necessary in order to produce beautiful art. Stone will always resist the sculptor, but that does not mean it cannot become a great work of art.

We live in an era in which people prefer to resist conflict, yet conflict is often a necessary part of change. As we prepare to issue our challenge, we want you to be open to change while you are also questioning us and the Bible we promote. It's okay for you to resist, but be careful about closing yourself off completely to the conflicts in your life, which are needed to mold you and shape you, to make you into the work of art you were always meant to be.

THE CHALLENGE

Lauren and I are competitive. We compete with each other. We compete with others. It's in our nature to rise to a good challenge. Recently, we were laughing about an example of our constant competitiveness. As we were walking up to Universal Studios (to visit Harry Potter World, of course!), there were multiple lines to present tickets and enter the park. Without discussing a plan, we instinctively went to separate lines, wanting to get in as fast as possible. We could better our chances of getting in quickly by splitting up and each joining the line that seemed fastest. We were competing against everyone else trying to get into the park, and as a team we knew we could win.

We inherited this trait from our families, both of whom favor an environment of healthy competition. We even competed with each other in the process of writing this book. It is this healthy competition that makes us stronger. We began this book by addressing three audiences—the Bible-readers, the Bible-open, and the Bible-closed—and we want to end by returning to these three audiences. We have a challenge for each of you.

FOR THE BIBLE-READERS

The first group we want to challenge are those who are Bible-readers, people who read the Bible regularly and believe the Bible is an important and essential part of life. If this is you, our challenge to you is to be open to wrestling with hard questions about the Bible. Poke and prod the Scriptures. Become a proper skeptic of what they say. If the Bible is what it claims to be, it can handle your fiercest line of questioning. As you wrestle with the Scriptures, you will become all the more familiar with them. We encourage you to be a thoughtful student of the Bible. We hope that our book can be a useful tool for this challenge and that you feel encouraged by our story and resonate with our experience. There will always be voices challenging your belief in the Bible, and temptations to reject it when it veers outside the boundaries of cultural norms. Are you willing to continue to engage with the Bible?

One of our favorite books is *Mere Christianity* by C. S. Lewis. In it he writes,

> Creatures are not born with desires unless satisfaction for those desires exists. A baby feels hunger: well, there is such a thing as food. A duckling wants to swim: well, there is such a thing as water. Men feel sexual desire: well, there is such a thing as sex. If I find in myself a desire which no experience in this world can satisfy, the most probable explanation is that I was made for another world. If none of my earthly pleasures satisfy it, that does not prove that the universe is a fraud. Probably earthly pleasures were never meant to satisfy it, but only to arouse it, to suggest the real thing. If that is so, I must take care, on the one

hand, never to despise, or to be unthankful for, these earthly blessings, and on the other, never to mistake them for the something else of which they are only a kind of copy, or echo, or mirage. I must keep alive in myself the desire for my true country, which I shall not find till after death; I must never let it get snowed under or turned aside; I must make it the main object of life to press on to that country and to help others to do the same.[4]

FOR THE BIBLE-OPEN

The second group we wish to challenge are those who are Bible-open. Those of you who are Bible-open have perhaps grown up in the church or have otherwise been exposed to the Bible, but for a variety of reasons you have stopped reading it or turning to it for guidance and comfort. Many of you are our friends, our former classmates, or former church members who were turned off by institutional religion. Many in this group will be familiar with some of the classic stories and concepts of the Bible.

We understand that for many of you, there is a deeper reason why you've turned away from the Bible. Most of the time, when people bring up the problems they have with the Bible, it really isn't about the Bible; it's about people. And this gets all too real, because people can do some real damage. Perhaps those who claim to believe the Bible have hurt or rejected you. If this is the case, let us, on behalf of other Christians, say how sorry we are that you experienced injustice. This book, and our challenge, is in no way meant to overlook or minimize the pain you experienced. Rather we want to point to the Book that holds wrongdoers accountable for what they've done to you. There are those who have misapplied the Bible for their own selfish gains, creating a wake of hurt for others. God will judge more strictly those who teach the Bible (James 3:1).

Some of you avoid the Bible because you are afraid of the conflict it may bring to your way of life. The Bible is not neutral; it is active and will challenge your assumptions about God, life, morals, ethics, and the future. The Danish philosopher Søren Kierkegaard once wrote, "The Bible is very easy to understand. But we Christians are a bunch of scheming swindlers. We pretend to be unable to understand it because we know very well that the minute we understand, we are obliged to act accordingly."[5] Often we seek to avoid something not because we believe it is false but because we are afraid of what it means if it is true. If you have avoided going to the doctor, you may understand this phenomenon.

Whether you have disengaged out of anger or avoidance, our challenge is this: Are you willing to give Jesus a chance? The Bible is not a set of rules, and it is not just good advice. The Bible is a story of good news about an invitation to have the relationship you need—a relationship between you and God that is made possible in Jesus Christ. The Bible paints a portrait of who Jesus is, how he lived, how he loved, and how he desires a relationship with you. We are not asking you to immediately accept his church or his followers, but are you willing to encounter Jesus himself? Are you willing to let him introduce himself as he truly is, as opposed to what people say about him? Regardless of your experience with those who claim the name Christian and claim to be doing Christ's work, are you willing to give Jesus a chance? If so, he is found in the pages of the Bible. Sit down with a copy yourself and begin anew this journey of discovering who he is and what he has done for you.

FOR THE BIBLE-CLOSED

The final group we want to challenge are the Bible-closed. These people have rejected religious affiliation altogether, and whether simply spiritual or decidedly atheist, they have no interest in the Bible. It's likely that at some point in this book, we have offended them. If you're in this group, we hope we have introduced some points of view that are novel and unique and have caused you to consider or reconsider the value of the Bible.

We must acknowledge that we have known some of the most genuine and caring people who would consider themselves to be in this category. Despite their active resistance to the Bible, they display loving-kindness to the world around them. They are sincere in their concern about the Bible's teachings, and they can be quick to admit their error when they are challenged in an argument. While not all are like this, many Bible-closed friends of ours display a better adherence to the Bible's ethical teachings than some who call themselves Christians.

To these Bible-closed readers and friends: We are not asking you to believe the Bible. We are not asking you to base your life on the Bible. We are not even asking you to believe that it possesses absolute truth. All we are asking of you is that you be open enough to read it. You are part of the open-minded generation; you have more information at your fingertips than anyone in human history. There is a chorus of voices and opinions that insist the Bible is outdated, that it is fantasy, fiction, myth, dangerous, and irrelevant. But are you willing, as Steve Jobs put it, to let "the noise of others' opinions drown out your own inner voice"?[6]

We get it. You have doubts. We have been there. Do you have

the courage to doubt your own doubts? If you do, you might find yourself catching a surprising truth.

Are you willing to enter a no-judgment zone and form an opinion for yourself? Do not rely on the media's portrayal of the Bible or the opinion of your college professors or even our opinion. Read it for yourself, and then form your own opinion.

We hope that by now you are motivated to begin reading the Bible and are asking yourself where to start. As we mentioned, the Bible is a diverse collection of sixty-six books. Both the Old Testament and the New Testament focus on God's plan to rescue the world through his chosen Messiah, Jesus. The books in the New Testament make it clear that Jesus is the key to unlocking the whole Bible. So if you want to read the Bible well, the first thing we recommend is that you get to know Jesus.

The life of Jesus was recorded by four different authors who either were eyewitnesses of the events of his life or interviewed eyewitnesses. The four books they wrote are referred to as the Gospels and are at the beginning of the New Testament. In the time you took to read this book, you could have read all four of the accounts from Matthew, Mark, Luke, and John. Matthew was a Jewish tax collector, one of Jesus' twelve closest followers. Mark records Peter's perspective of Jesus' life. Luke was a doctor who spoke with many of Jesus' early followers and was discipled by Paul. John was Jesus' best friend on earth.

We understand that engaging with the Bible may be uncomfortable, but enter into dialogue with the Bible anyway. After all, we are the open-minded generation, ready and willing to try anything once. So why not give the Bible a chance? We freely admit that there are many who are Bible engaged, like us, but who associate only with others who share their perspective on the Bible. There are also many who are Bible-closed who interact only with others who find the Bible to be a hilarious waste of time. We hope this book can begin a dialogue between people about the Bible, regardless of whether you love the Bible, hate the Bible, or are somewhere in between.

We hope to see conversations sparked in which we can be honest about our doubts, our questions, and our appreciation of the Bible. Just as I (Michael) had to experience Harry Potter for myself to grasp the excitement and obsession surrounding the bestselling fictional series, read the Bible's true story for yourself to grasp the life-changing implications of the world's number one bestseller.

Read the Bible for yourself. With humility and curiosity, engage with this Book that has transformed the world. Set aside people's failures and don't hold them against the Bible. Every person you know will let you down, including yourself. But the God of the Bible has proved in our lives to be a perfect Father and a constant source of hope, joy, and peace. We invite you to be open-minded enough to open his Book and give him an opportunity to prove to be the same for you.

NOTES

Chapter 1: Are We Missing Out?

1. "Internet Growth Statistics," Internet World Stats (September 3, 2018), *www.internetworldstats.com/emarketing.htm*.
2. Barna Group and American Bible Society, *The Bible in America: The Changing Landscape of Bible Perceptions and Engagement* (Ventura, CA: Barna Group, 2016), 101.
3. Ibid., 25.
4. Ibid., 111.
5. "State of the Bible in 2017: Top Findings," Barna Group (April 4, 2017), *www.barna.com/research/state-bible-2017-top-findings/*.
6. Barna Group and American Bible Society, *The Bible in America: The Changing Landscape of Bible Perceptions and Engagement* (Barna Group, 2016), 111.

Chapter 2: What Is a Millennial? The Five I's

1. "Gallup Analysis: Millennials, Marriage and Family," Gallup (May 19, 2016), *http://news.gallup.com/poll/191462/gallup-analysis-millennials-marriage-family.aspx*.
2. Jeffrey Jensen Arnett, "From Emerging Adulthood to Young Adulthood: The Big Picture," NEFE Symposium (November 2008), *www.nefe.org/Portals/0/WhatWeProvide/PrimaryResearch/PDF/YA_Arnett_Presentation.pdf?ver=2012–04–17–191818–000*.
3. Amy Adkins, "What Millennials Want from Work and Life," Gallup (May 10, 2016), *http://news.gallup.com/businessjournal/*

*191435/millennials-work-life.aspx?g_source=position1&g_medium
=related&g_campaign=tiles.*

4. Barna Group and American Bible Society, *The Bible in America:
   The Changing Landscape of Bible Perceptions and Engagement*
   (Barna Group, 2016), 141–42.

5. Christine Barton, Jeff Fromm, and Chris Egan, "The Millennial
   Consumer: Debunking Stereotypes," Boston Consulting Group
   (April 2012), *www.bcg.com/documents/file103894.pdf*, 4.

6. Jess Rainer and Thom S. Rainer, *The Millennials: Connecting to
   America's Largest Generation* (Nashville: B&H, 2011), 13–14.

7. The exact number fluctuates, depending on the source: some consider
   the birth date range for millennials to be 1981–1998 and place
   the number of millennials at closer to 75 million; others consider
   the range to be 1980–2000 and place the number at 78 million.
   Regardless of how it is measured, the millennial generation is
   larger than any previous generation.

8. Fred Dews, "Eleven Facts about the Millennial Generation,"
   Brookings Institution (June 2, 2014), *www.brookings.edu/blog/brook
   ings-now/2014/06/02/11-facts-about-the-millennial-generation/*.

9. Barton, Fromm, and Egan, "Millennial Consumer," 5.

10. "Millennials Are Hardly Newsless, Uninterested, or Disengaged
    from News and the World around Them," American Press Institute
    (March 16, 2015), *www.americanpressinstitute.org/publications/
    reports/survey-research/millennials-not-newsless/*; Barton, Fromm,
    and Egan, "Millennial Consumer," 5.

11. "Millennials Are Hardly Newsless," American Press Institute.

12. Barton, Fromm, and Egan, "Millennial Consumer," 8.

13. Ibid.

14. Barton, Fromm, and Egan, "The Millennial Consumer," 6.

15. Morgan Housel, "The Difference between Impatience and Having
    No Tolerance for Inefficiency," Collaborative Fund (January 4,
    2017), *www.collaborativefund.com/blog/the-difference-between
    -impatience-and-having-no-tolerance-for-inefficiency/*.

16. Rainer and Rainer, *Millennials*, 36–37.

17. Barton, Fromm, and Egan, "Millennial Consumer," 7.

18. "Millennials—Breaking the Myths," Nielsen (2014), *www.explore*

midtown.org/wp-content/uploads/2015/04/nielsen-millennial-report
-feb-2014.pdf, 12.

19. Dews, "Eleven Facts about the Millennial Generation."
20. "Millennials—Breaking the Myths," Nielsen, 12.
21. "Meet the Millennial Multicultural Music Listener," Nielsen (August 25, 2014), *www.nielsen.com/us/en/insights/news/2014/ meet-the-millennial-multicultural-music-listener.print.html.*
22. "Mobile Fact Sheet," Pew Research Center (February 5, 2018), *http://www.pewinternet.org/fact-sheet/mobile/.*
23. "Millennials—Breaking the Myths," Nielsen, 35.
24. Barton, Fromm, and Egan, "Millennial Consumer," 5.

Chapter 3: Our Problem with Truth

1. "How Millennials Want to Live and Work," Gallup (September 1, 2018), *http://news.gallup.com/reports/189830/e.aspx.*
2. Christine Barton, Jeff Fromm, and Chris Egan, "The Millennial Consumer: Debunking Stereotypes," Boston Consulting Group (April 2012), *www.bcg.com/documents/file103894.pdf*, 6.
3. Ibid.
4. James Davison Hunter, *To Change the World: The Irony, Tragedy, and Possibility of Christianity in the Late Modern World* (New York: Oxford, 2010), 33.
5. Christian Smith, *Soul Searching: The Religious and Spiritual Lives of American Teenagers* (Oxford: Oxford Univ. Press, 2005), 47.
6. Ibid., 48.
7. Ibid., 50.

Chapter 4: What Is the Bible's Message?

1. Barna Group and American Bible Society, *The Bible in America: The Changing Landscape of Bible Perceptions and Engagement* (Barna Group, 2016), 25.
2. Ibid., 23.
3. Richard Dawkins, "Why I Want All Our Children to Read the King James Bible," *Guardian* (May 2012), *www.theguardian.com/ science/2012/may/19/richard-dawkins-king-james-bible.*
4. Tim Keller, "Jesus Vindicated," *Christianity Today* (September 1,

2018), *www.preachingtoday.com/sermons/sermons/2014/march/*
jesus-vindicated.html.

5. Barna Group and ABS, *The Bible in America*, 48.

Chapter 5: Millennials and History

1. Reid Wilson, "More Millennials Living with Parents," *Hill*
   (April 24, 2017), *http://thehill.com/homenews/state-watch/330279*
   -more-millennials-living-with-parents.
2. Bella DePaulo, "Why Are So Many Young Adults Living with
   Their Parents?" *Psychology Today* (May 26, 2016), *www.psychology*
   today.com/us/blog/living-single/201605/why-are-so-many-young
   -adults-living-their-parents.
3. Wikisource, "The Encyclopedia Americana (1920) / American Bible
   Society, The," *https://en.wikisource.org/wiki/The_Encyclopedia_*
   Americana_(1920)/American_Bible_Society,_The.
4. "Religion among the Millennials," Pew Research Center
   (February 17, 2010), *www.pewforum.org/2010/02/17/religion*
   -among-the-millennials/; "State of the Bible in 2017: Top Findings,"
   Barna Group (April 4, 2017), *www.barna.com/research/state-bible*
   -2017-top-findings/.
5. Joel Stein, "Millennials: The Me Me Me Generation," *Time*, May 20,
   2013, *http://time.com/247/millennials-the-me-me-me-generation/*.
6. "Religion among the Millennials," Pew Research Center.
7. Ibid.

Chapter 6: The Bible's Impact

1. "Human Rights: What Are Human Rights?" United Nations, *www*
   .un.org/en/sections/issues-depth/human-rights/.
2. Scott R. Paeth, E. Harold Breitenberg Jr., and Hak Joon Lee,
   Shaping Public Theology: Selections from the Writings of Max L.
   Stackhouse (Grand Rapids: Eerdmans, 2014), 275.
3. Martin Luther King Jr., "Letter from a Birmingham Jail," August 1963,
   3, *https://web.cn.edu/kwheeler/documents/Letter_Birmingham_Jail.pdf*.
4. While many would attribute this freedom to a secular
   enlightenment rooted in the humanism of the seventeenth and
   eighteenth centuries, we would argue that religious freedom finds
   its source in Scripture.

Chapter 7: What Makes the Bible Unique?

1. "The Battle of the Books," *Economist* (December 19, 2007), *www .economist.com/node/10311317*.
2. "The Bible in America: Six-Year Trends," Barna Group (June 15, 2016), *www.barna.com/research/the-bible-in-america-6-year-trends/*.
3. Paul records in a letter to one of his partners in ministry, Timothy, that "all Scripture is breathed out by God and profitable for teaching, for reproof, for correction, and for training in righteousness, that the man of God may be complete, equipped for every good work" (2 Tim. 3:16–17 ESV).
4. "The Bible in America: Six-Year Trends," Barna Group.
5. Ibid.

Chapter 8: Should I Read at All?

1. A. G. Sertillanges, *The Intellectual Life* (Cork, Ireland: Catholic Univ. Press, 1987), 151.
2. Andrew Perrin, "Book Reading 2016: Appendix A," Pew Research Center (September 1, 2016), *www.pewinternet.org/2016/09/01/book-reading-2016-appendix-a/*.
3. Neil Gaiman, "Why Our Future Depends on Libraries, Reading, and Daydreaming," *Guardian* (October 15, 2013), *www.theguardian.com/books/2013/oct/15/neil-gaiman-future-libraries-reading-daydreaming*.

Chapter 10: The Bible and Spirituality

1. "The Bible in America: Six-Year Trends," Barna Group (June 15, 2016), *www.barna.com/research/the-bible-in-america-6-year-trends/*.
2. Sam Harris, *Waking Up: A Guide to Spirituality without Religion* (New York: Simon and Schuster, 2014), 7.
3. D. A. Carson, ed., *The Scriptures Testify about Me: Jesus and the Gospel in the Old Testament* (Wheaton, IL: Crossway, 2013), 44.

Chapter 11: How to Start

1. Many scholars would divide this into two sections: the first five books of the Bible are called the Torah, or Pentateuch.
2. R. C. Sproul, *Knowing Scripture* (Downers Grove, IL: InterVarsity, 1977), 17.
3. LW 35:236.

Notes

Chapter 12: The Challenge

1. Anya Kamenetz, "Half of Professors in NPR Ed Survey Have Used 'Trigger Warnings,'" NPR (September 7, 2016), *www.npr.org/sections/ed/2016/09/07/492979242/half-of-professors-in-npr-ed-survey-have-used-trigger-warnings*.
2. Alan Levinovitz, "How Trigger Warnings Silence Religious Students," *Atlantic* (August 30, 2016), *www.theatlantic.com/politics/archive/2016/08/silencing-religious-students-on-campus/497951/*.
3. Ibid.
4. C. S. Lewis, *Mere Christianity* (New York: Harper One, 1952), 136–37.
5. Søren Kierkegaard, *Provocations: Spiritual Writings of Kierkegaard* (Walden, NY: Plough, 2002), 197.
6. Steve Jobs, Stanford University commencement speech (2005).